Success Factors of Young African American Women at a Historically Black College

Success Factors of Young African American Women at a Historically Black College

Marilyn J. Ross

PRAEGER

Westport, Connecticut
London

Library of Congress Cataloging-in-Publication Data

Ross, Marilyn J.
  Success factors of young African American women at a historically black college
/ Marilyn J. Ross.
    p. cm.
  Includes bibliographical references and index.
  ISBN 0-89789-737-4 (alk. paper)
    1. African American women—Education (Higher). 2. African American college
students—Social conditions. 3. African American universities and colleges.
4. Academic achievement—United States. I. Title.
  LC2781 .R665 2003
  378.1′9829′96073—dc21   2002029880

British Library Cataloguing in Publication Data is available.

Library of Congress Catalog Card Number: 2002029880
ISBN: 0-89789-737-4

First published in 2003

Praeger Publishers, 88 Post Road West, Westport, CT 06881
An imprint of Greenwood Publishing Group, Inc.
www.praeger.com

Printed in the United States of America

The paper used in this book complies with the
Permanent Paper Standard issued by the National
Information Standards Organization (Z39.48-1984).

10 9 8 7 6 5 4 3 2 1

To
Michael I. Ross,
my husband and best friend,

and
to our family,
Sharyn Leslie and Jeffrey, Kathryn Anya and Alexander
Forrest, Andrew Dean and Andee Hope, Miller Shea,
Scarlett Rae, and Daschle Gray

with all my love

Contents

Acknowledgments

I wish to recognize all those women students who gave their dedication and time in the interest of furthering scholarship through the interview process. I wish to recognize those students who critiqued the writings of African American women and expressed the importance of the words in their own lives: Khalia Jelks, Khalelah Patterson, Michael Lang, Bridget Gibbs, and Amy Rae. I wish to recognize Shekeetha Law for the introductory inscription. I wish to recognize the students in my Women's Writers classes, who gave me feedback on themes discovered; my students were my collaborators. I wish to recognize Kiwan Harrison and the help, enthusiasm, and constancy that he showed me during the time that he was a student at Florida Memorial College.

I wish to recognize the various libraries that I used: Florida Memorial College Library, Schomburg Center for Research and Black Culture in Harlem, Humanities and Social Science section of the New York Research Library, Mid-Manhattan Library, Florida International Library, and University of Miami Library. I wish to recognize the depth and breadth of the archive section of Florida Memorial College Library. I wish to recognize the Florida Memorial College librarians, who took the time and effort to help me in my search for relevant material.

I wish to recognize Dr. William Hopper, Director of Institutional Research, Florida Memorial College, for up-to-date demographic data on the college. I wish to recognize longtime friend and colleague Dr. Sandra T. Thompson, Assistant Provost and Professor of Sociology, Florida Memorial College, for always being there for advice and encouragement. I wish to acknowledge Jane Garry, acquisitions editor, Greenwood Publishing Group, for having confidence in the project.

And I wish to recognize my husband and best friend, Michael I. Ross, who always demonstrates strong support and caring, whose interest never wavers, and who edited the final draft.

Introduction

Home of Discretion

So what! I keep quiet and let what happens in a household
Stay in a household;

To only find out the happiest day of my life
Is yet to be told;

I don't understand how home can be where the heart is
If this is not my world;

I've seen things that should only be kept secret
Not told to anyone, especially a deacon;

That's when I keep quiet and let what happens in a household
Stay in a household;

To only find out that the happiest day of my life
Is yet to be told.

Shekeetha Law (2002)

PRESENT: AFRICAN AMERICAN COLLEGE STUDENTS (2002)

Little, if any, research has been done on African American women who successfully steered themselves through the streets of inner city neighborhoods and who attend college. Their personal stories and struggles go unheard. Yet knowledge of their ability to circumvent difficult obstacles in growing up would be of value for other young women to follow. Recording their life stories and the strand of determination that links African American women historically is the basis of this study.

These young women's experiences have been harrowing, involving single-parent homes, inner city violence, and responsibilities beyond their years. Through this research, I learned that no one can conjecture what another person's life experiences have been. Casual conversation does not tell the story; newspaper accounts do not grasp the totality of an event. I thought I knew my students and their circumstances, but only when I started to develop case studies did I realize that I didn't know them at all. Yet their circumstances and difficulties seemed mundane to them. Through candid accounts in lengthy interview sessions, I learned about the obstacles that they had to overcome in growing up. I also realized the inner strength they needed to persevere. I feel this information is worth sharing with the community.

The oral narrative has always been an important part of black culture. The African legacy has been handed down through the ages by storytellers, called *griots,* who were similar to the bards of ancient Greece and Rome. These philosophical poets kept traditions alive through oral chants; today, folk singers, "rappers," and street corner "brothers" hand down contemporary cultural phenomena. The past and the present have a curious way of coming together in black culture.

Oral history has become an important research tool. It is a primary source for establishing firsthand impressions within a historical time frame. The women that I interviewed grew up in an inner city environment in the 1990s. By narrating the disadvantages that they had overcome, they were not only facing their emotions head-on, but they were also sharing with others the difficult road they had traveled to reach an important destination in their lives: *college*. Their successful milestones could serve as an inspiration for others to emulate.

However, this study is more than the highlighting of archetypes of survival for other women to learn from; this study is relevant because these women, who have overcome formidable obstacles, bring enlightenment to themselves—the awareness that they have turned a corner into the independence that is required of them in the African American community.

At this stage, they are mature enough to make their own decisions. Psychologically and physically, they are away from the fray. At this juncture, they know they will not be a part of the hapless many and the multilevel dangers of the inner city. They are safe.

Black women are the lifeline of their community. This sample group, through the education that they are pursuing and the professionalism that they will gain, will help fulfill the community's expectations: to uplift their race. That conviction has always been at the heart of the black community, documented in black women's organizations and the ideology of the black church. These young women have demonstrated that they know their role in life and have accepted it.

FOCUS AND PARADIGM OF THE STUDY

This study examines life experiences of young African American women who were born and raised in the inner city and who, at present, still call that neighborhood their home. These women are a product of predominantly single-parent homes and lower-income families. Because of the specificity of choosing the sample, I want to state that the findings are pertinent to the cluster selected and cannot be generalized to include the entire population of African American women. This study, therefore, should be seen as the life experiences of a specific group of African American women, and the suppositions inscribed in it should not be used to describe the status of African American women universally.

METHODS OF INQUIRY

This research is based on the methodology of naturalistic inquiry, which is qualitative in nature. Qualitative research has been accepted in higher education and sociological studies for many decades. It is especially relevant in minority studies, because of the powerlessness of the subjects to get their voices heard. The emerging truths are verified through various methods, for example, triangulation, peer critiquing, and negative case analysis (Lincoln and Guba, 1985; Vaz (ed.), 1997; Ross, 1998). In this case, I used *triangulation* to corroborate the data:

1. Findings and analysis of the study were made available in my office for respondents to review the accuracy of the transcribed interviews, to discuss emerging themes, and to give feedback.
2. Male and female members of the English Club, 2000–2002, read the study as it progressed, discussed issues, and supported the outcome.
3. When studying African American women writers in the classroom, idiosyncratic cultural descriptions from the interviews were discussed and verified by students, who were of the same culture.

All feedback was taken into consideration.

The practice of *peer debriefing* (analysis of findings by colleagues) is another validity check in qualitative research. This was practiced in the following manner:

1. During a seminar on the African diaspora (2001) held at Florida Memorial College, I presented a report of my findings. Professors from local and Caribbean universities in the fields of anthropology, history, psychology, sociology, and English critiqued and accepted the suppositions I postulated.
2. Dr. Sandra T. Thompson, professor of sociology, Florida Memorial College, read segments of the study and gave guidance and critical feedback.

Proof of the data by reliable sources gives validity to the study and is an important part of verifying truth. Both triangulation and peer debriefing fit the guidelines for sound qualitative research.

The term *negative case analysis* refers to a process for refining the hypothesis—an in-depth analysis of all facts—so that the researcher can forthrightly set out his or her claim that all evidence, without exception, is in agreement with the stated theory (Ross, 1998, p. 31).

Researchers should be aware that the results of a qualitative study may not be easily replicated. However, as this study was framed by an explicit set of questions and qualifying factors, one can conjecture that this research and its methods could be duplicated in another sample with similar statistics.

THE RESEARCH PROCESS

The first step in the research process was to select the sample. Although there is a group on campus called "The First Lady's Women" (a group comparable to "The President's Men," the sample used in my 1998 study on male students), the group consisted of predominantly Caribbean students. That would not work; I was interested in interviewing African American women generally. After exploring several options, I realized that many of the women students who had previously been in my classes fit the project's criteria. They were also the most interested in participating and the most reliable in keeping their interview appointments. They became the core group of the sample.

I followed the same path of discovery as in my book on male students:

1. I selected the sample according to the criteria that were set forth;
2. I explained the research to each student on an individual, private basis;
3. I reviewed important aspects of qualitative research with them so that the process itself would be a learning experience;
4. I kept an audit trail of the study in individual files:
   - transcribed case study;
   - informed consent document;
   - biographical profile form;
   - microcassette tape of the interview.

SELECTION OF THE SAMPLE AND INTERVIEW QUESTIONS

As a complement and sequel to my book, *Success Factors of Young African American Males at a Historically Black College* (1998), I selected a sample of twenty women college students to ascertain the similarities and differences of obstacles that they had to overcome in order to reach this level of attainment. In order to become one of the sample group, each student had to meet criteria similar to those of the male students in *success* factors.

1. students born and raised in an inner city environment;
2. maximum age of twenty-five years old;
3. minimum 3.0 grade-point average;
4. junior status at the college.

The women were selected after determining that they matched the prerequisites. Many were former students of mine, and they knew me as professor and advisor. This became key in their trust of me. Several had perused the book on young male college students and wanted to participate in a similar book about women.

Ten basic questions were asked of each of the twenty women, eight of the ten were identical to the questions asked of the men. All of the interviews were developed into holistic case studies. Only when the questioning period was reduced to redundancy did I feel that I had fulfilled the essentials necessary for authenticity. The interviewing session generally lasted one hour and resulted in interviews of approximately ten typed pages, single-spaced, comparable in length to the men's case studies. An Olympus Pearlcorder L400 microcassette recorder was used to tape both women's and men's interviews, and an Olympus T1010 transcriber was used to transcribe all the interviews.

The following eight interview questions were asked of each group (women and men):

1. What factors do you identify as contributing to your success?
2. What factors do you identify as obstacles to your success?
3. Who/what were the major influences in your life?
4. What activities and organizations do you identify as being important to your development?
5. What thoughts pass through your mind when making a decision?
6. What is inside you that motivates you to succeed?
7. How do you define success?
8. What recommendations do you have for youngsters in the community?

Two additional questions were asked of the women:

9. Have you experienced any violence in your neighborhood when growing up?
10. From your perspective, why do young teenagers have babies out of wedlock?

PERSPECTIVES ON QUALITATIVE/NARRATIVE RESEARCH

I conduct my own interviews. I do not believe that I could get adequate results if someone else did this very important part of the research. In qualitative investigation, the respondents are the most important link in establishing truth. The elemental truths are grounded in the spoken word, the individual's interpretation of his or her own world.

SIGNIFICANT FACTORS FOR THE SOUNDNESS OF THE RESEARCH

Significant factors in ascertaining the soundness of the research include the following:

1. minimum number in the sample: twelve individuals (Lincoln and Guba, 1985);
2. triangulation: confirmation of themes and collected data by a group "insider," who is deemed reliable to assess the information;
3. prolonged engagement and persistent observation: I have been a member of the faculty for thirty-one years. Additionally, an important resource for this book is the research that I completed for a book on young men (Ross, 1998), seventeen of whom came from similar circumstances to the young women;
4. no a priori assumptions: the qualitative researcher has no prior theories about the study.

The study is inductive in nature; the information is collected bit by bit. The eventual research design can be envisioned as pyramid shaped and broad based, with many propositions to consider. These possible issues need to be integrated into a meaningful thesis that explains the fundamental reality of the problem being investigated.

CATEGORIZING THE EMERGING THEMES: IDENTIFYING UNITS

When the interview process was complete, I reviewed the case studies for emerging concepts and made notes of my thoughts in the margins. I then separated distinct categories and listed direct quotations from the transcribed interviews as supporting evidence (see student reflections on "mothers," "single motherhood," "grandmothers," "fathers," "violence," "church," "peer pressure," "abuse," "goal-setting," and "advice to young black women in the community" in Chapter 4). In this way, categories are coupled with the spoken word. In this study, through the images presented, I could figuratively see, touch, and feel the world of the respondents. The inferences are grounded in the respondents' words—their own reality, an important aspect of qualitative or narrative inquiry (Ross, 1998, pp. 32–35).

In order to fully interpret a "strange" culture, the researcher immerses him- or herself in the setting, similar to an anthropologist, and "becomes" a part of the culture (Crabtree and Miller, 1992, p. 24). He or she is the "human instrument" of analysis and becomes sensitive to the gestalt of the situation in an attempt to untangle the mystery of "What is happening here?" (Ross, 1998, p. 21). What are the causes? What are the effects?

Becoming a participant-observer in the field is a significant component of the investigation. In essence, the successful researcher needs an inquisitive nature, intuitive sensibility, and patience over time (prolonged engagement) to *construct reality* from an accumulation of data (Lincoln and Guba, 1985; Crabtree and Miller, 1992; Ross, 1998).

NARROWING THE HYPOTHESIS

In qualitative research, the final hypothesis evolves over time. Tentative theories are drawn throughout the study, but only through dogged perseverance and faithful immersion in the culture, will the researcher feel secure that his/her final analysis "fits" the circumstance. Glaser and Strauss (1967) assert that:

> By the close of his investigation, [the researcher's] conviction about his theory would be hard to shake. . . . The fieldworker knows what he knows, not only because he's been there in the field and because of his careful verification of hypotheses, but because "in his bones" he feels the worth of his final analysis. (p. 58)

Throughout the process, one can utilize strategies to corroborate tentative theories: for example, (a) "look at everyday practices, not just beliefs about those practices"; (b) objectively examine "background conditions, such as immediate context, social practices, personal histories, shared practices, and language" (Addison, 1992, pp. 111, 112); (c) compare data across case studies, termed the *constant comparative method;* (d) seek out disagreements in data to refine assumptions, termed *negative case analysis;* (e) take field notes including *rich descriptions* of the individuals and setting; (f) review each day's accumulation of data (Glaser and Strauss, 1967; Lincoln and Guba, 1985; Crabtree and Miller, 1992; Vaz, 1997a; Ross, 1998).

In order to establish valid results, the researcher must determine overriding impressions that link *all* the data. In this study, the overriding impression is the *haunting silence* of being *alone*.

SETTING

The setting of this study is a four-year liberal arts college established in 1879 subsequent to the Civil War, for the vocational training of blacks to prepare them to enter society as freedmen. Interracial contacts through Baptist organizations became part of the historical legacy of the college. Both black and white Baptist ministers were united in this educational effort to instruct previously enslaved children and their progeny. This thrust became a Christian mission.

With the strong leadership of the Baptists, the school grew from its modest beginnings as a vocational training institute to the four-year, multifaceted college that it is today. Through the years, it has met the challenges of change and renewal.

The origin of the college is deeply rooted in the strength symbolized by a feature of the natural environment in Live Oak, Florida, the oak tree. Its growth came slowly. Two institutions: the Florida Baptist Institute, Live Oak, 1879, and the Florida Baptist Academy, Jacksonville, 1892, merged in 1941 to form the Florida Normal and Industrial Memorial Institute in a new setting, St. Augustine, Florida. The institution flourished into four-year college status in 1945, and, eventually, through various name changes, the present name Florida Memorial College was adopted in 1963. Because of racial unrest in St. Augustine and the necessity of seeking out more opportunities for the school and its students, in 1968 the college moved to its present urban location, Miami, Florida.

The culture of the college is unique. This 123-year-old historically black college is a composite of students, faculty, and staff who could very well be the descendants of those kidnapped men, women, and children brought from the east coast of Africa to various places in the New World and divers islands off the coast of Florida. This integration of students and faculty brings to the campus insights and experiences of the African diaspora, which lends itself to sharing feelings and belief systems in a stimulating intellectual climate.

Florida Memorial College's Institutional Statement of Purpose emphasizes its dedication to the free exchange of ideas and the transmission and preservation of African American history and heritage. The definitive mission statement includes the importance of instilling in students the pursuit of life-long learning, character, and commitment to leadership through service—to raise the quality of one's life and the lives of others.

Black colleges nationwide set a vision and a goal for underprivileged youth from the inner city. Black colleges are student-oriented; they guide the young into technical and professional careers. I have been a member of the faculty since 1971, three years after the college relocated in Miami from St. Augustine. I have seen the college grow academically in the number of Ph.Ds hired, programs offered, technical equipment installed, and buildings erected. I have been fortunate in sharing in the lives of thousands of youths, and I have seen Florida Memorial College's administrators, faculty, and staff make selfless efforts to give these youths an opportunity to share in the American dream.

Florida Memorial College has been successful in its efforts. Graduates have become leaders in the community. They are doctors, lawyers, scientists, social scientists, public administrators, entrepreneurs, computer analysts, and pilots. The various academic divisions include: Airway and Computer Sciences, Business Administration, Education, Extension and Continuing Education, General College Division, Humanities, Natural Sciences and Mathematics, and Social Sciences.

The ethnic composition of the school has always been diverse. It varies; for example, in the 1980s, when I was producing cross-cultural programming for Florida Memorial College on educational television, the students at the college represented cultures and countries such as Saudi Arabia, Nigeria, South Africa, Ethiopia, and Eritrea; Florida Memorial College has always been a place where people of color bonded in an effort to further their education.

Currently, the gender and ethnic composition of the student body, as compiled, in a booklet of the same name, by the the Office of Institutional Research (March 2002), is less global. The school's student body is comprised of students who come from the United States, Caribbean, and Hispanic community in Miami:

Nonresident aliens	217
Black, non-Hispanic/African American	1,862
Hispanic	66
White, non-Hispanic	8
Other	1

The demographic terms, as listed here, have been established by the United States Department of Education:

Nonresident aliens: those students, generally from the Bahamas, Jamaica, St. Thomas, Haiti, and other nearby islands off the coast of Miami, who are not a citizen or national of the United States and who are in the country on a visa or temporary basis; they do not have the right to remain indefinitely.

Black, non-Hispanic: a person having origins in any of the black racial groups of Africa (except those of Hispanic origin); African American.

Hispanic: a person of Mexican, Puerto Rican, Cuban, Central or South American, or other Spanish culture or origin, regardless of race.

White, non-Hispanic: a person having origins in any of the original peoples of Europe, North Africa, or the Middle East (except those of Hispanic origin).

Historically Black Colleges/Universities (HBCU): Colleges and universities that were established for the purpose of educating black youth at the postsecondary level.

The following table reflects the distribution of U.S. and Virgin Islands students enrolled at Florida Memorial College, 2001–2002:

Florida	1,550
Michigan	20
Illinois	19
Virgin Islands	58
Georgia	19
Other	270
Total U.S.	1,936
Percentage of students from Florida	80.1%

Source: Documented by the Office of Institutional Research (2002).

To more fully comprehend the milieu, it would be beneficial to examine a semester sample of the women and men who matriculate at the college. In the fall semester 2001, the total number of students enrolled was 2,154 (1,389 women, 765 men). Therefore, the percentage of black women enrolled was 64 percent; the percentage of black men enrolled was 36 percent, and the student body consisted of 624 more women than men.

These figures have a similar bearing on the emerging picture of *success* factors of women to men in the black community. In 1998, the published reports showed that "black men are falling behind black women in almost every assessment of progress in higher education" (Ross, 1998, p. 13). In the *Journal of Blacks in Higher Education* Winter 2001–2002 issue, the published index reveals the statistical breakdown of bachelor's degrees earned by African Americans, which documents that "Black women now earn approximately two thirds of all bachelor's degrees earned by African Americans" (p. 101). In the same issue, figures show that black women were awarded 68,520 bachelor's degrees, almost double earned by black men, who were awarded 35,638 bachelor's degrees (Cross, 2001–2, pp. 100–101).

Nationally, the imbalance between the number of black women college graduates and number of black men college graduates has a sociological effect: as recorded in the *Journal of Blacks in Higher Education*, Autumn 2001, the "success of black women compared to black men" (Cross and Slater, 2001, p. 102) is on the rise, resulting in black women equalizing income levels and "closing the income gap between college-educated blacks and whites"

(Cross, 2001, p. 33). Black women, therefore, continue to be the backbone of the black community.

Furthermore, the acceptance and gainful employment of black women over black men creates problems within female and male relationships, particularly feelings of worthlessness within the psyche of the black male. Oftentimes, his conscious or subconscious need to show manliness manifests itself in physical aggression, which can lead to estrangement from family life and society. Low enrollment and low graduation rates of black males at Florida Memorial College is an indicator of the plight of the black male in American society and the ensuing difficulties wrought upon black women.

The following figures show household family incomes of Florida Memorial College (FMC) students (Fall 2001) in comparison with students at other colleges and universities:

	FMC Students	Other College Students
Annual household income of less than $30,000	59%	12%
Annual household income of $30,000–49,999	20%	17%
Annual household income of $50,000 or more	21%	71%

Source: Cooperative Institutional Research Program, *The American Freshmen* (2001).

The analysis of student demographics by the college's Office of Institutional Research (2002) also reveals other disparities between Florida Memorial College students and other college students:

Indicator	FMC Percentage	National Percentage
Mother has college degree	16%	49%
Father has college degree	14%	52%
Student lives with both parents	27%	75%
Sudent expects significant family financial assistance	20%	64%
Student works full time	10%	3%

Note: Students who work full time take longer to graduate—on the average, six years.
Source: Office of Institutional Research (2002).

Florida Memorial College is a microcosm of the challenges facing inner city youth nationwide.

2

Review of the Literature

INSIGHTS FROM EXPERIENCE

Within the context of American culture and history, I will address the complex lives of black women in America. In my research published as *Success Factors of Young African American Males at a Historically Black College* (1998), I discovered that the success stories of the young men I studied were the result of a strong mother and/or grandmother who were the backbone and lifeline of the family. The literature acknowledges that black women have had the heaviest burden to bear within the African American community. If we contemplate the history of African American women from the period of slavery, we can easily claim that they have endured the greatest suffering of any group of people in American history. African American women should be studied within the context of their silent suffering and courageous overcoming.

As an English professor, I have learned that the feelings and experiences of people are best communicated by the people themselves. Therefore, we need to "hear" about yesterday through the "voices" of the past. In researching the experiences of black women during and after the time of slavery, I discovered that A. J. Cooper (1892), in *A Voice from the South,* expressed the same thought:

> that muffled chord, the one mute and voiceless note has been the sadly expectant Black Woman. . . . The "other side" has not been represented by one who "lives there." And not many can more sensibly realize and more accurately tell the weight and the fret of the "long dull pain" than the open-eyed but hitherto voiceless Black Woman of America. (pp. 1, 2)

For that purpose, I will combine first-person literary expressions discovered in archival collections, anthologies, journals, and documents within the context of the American experience; I also depict the hardships and obstacles faced by young African American women today as revealed in interviews with women college students. Is there a connection between the past and the present? I believe that the black woman has undergone the most aberrant experiences of any American, and through my experiences with women students in thirty-one years of classroom teaching at Florida Memorial College, a historically black college, I realize that the past humiliations of race and color remain an indelible part of the consciousness of the African American woman. The pain of the past is the pain of the present; it is a "long dull pain." It is so real that we can conjecture that the black woman today sees the world through flashbacks of other eras. Carl Jung's concept of the "collective unconscious" is at work within the black cultural milieu.

Double Consciousness

Black women have seen the world through a "double consciousness," comprising the consciousness of Self and the consciousness of Other. "Other" can be defined as the world without "hue," as delineated by "Whiteness." This is the world that constrains. W. E. B. DuBois early on used the concept of "double-consciousness" when he discussed the problem of black identity within the circumference of a white-ruled society. In *The Souls of Black Folk* (1961), he wrote, "one ever feels his twoness; two souls, two thoughts, two strivings; two [warring] ideals in one dark body, whose dogged strength alone keeps it from being torn asunder" (p. 102). In a more recent account, Wade-Gayles (1995) describes the black woman sitting cramped in a dark innermost circle, experiencing "pain, isolation, and vulnerability" (p. xix).

In one circle white people, mainly males, experience influence and power. Far removed from it is the second circle, a narrow space in which black people, regardless of sex, experience uncertainty and powerlessness. And in this narrow space, often hidden but no less present and real, is a small dark enclosure for black women only; it is in this enclosure that black women experience . . . the unique marks of black womanhood. (pp. xxvi–ii)

The term *double consciousness* is also often used to describe the psyche of a colonized people whose cultural beliefs are "reconstructed" in order to integrate the new political system. As reflected in the literature, the concept of reconstruction and the theme of identity remain an integral part of the black woman's life. From the beginning of black women's utterances in America, one can sense feelings of "loss" and a desire to become rooted. N. J. Burgess (1994), in her research titled "Gender Roles Revisited" records that

> Coupled with African cultural values and belief systems ... enslaved Africans were forced to embrace outwardly new rules, values, and roles. Family scholars suggest that traces of their African heritage continue to exist in the daily lives of African Americans, including the link for understanding current roles (p. 393).

Listening to and transcribing the interviews of young black women college students, I discovered that black women's lives have never become "whole." They remain "shattered," just as black men's lives are controlled by the American way for blacks—the sea of racism that never abates. In examining the legacy of racism, one can see the trail of discrimination, hopelessness, and unfulfilled lives. It is a dismal present arising from a dismal past. This heritage results in the black woman's constant struggle for the survival of self, family, and race.

In my research on the African American male "in crisis" (*Success Factors of Young African American Males at a Historically Black College*, 1998), a significant theme emerged—the theme of fear. In particular, this involved mothers' and grandmothers' fear for the safety of their children in an inner city environment. This impression remained a constant throughout the study.

Fear Permeates the Black Woman's Life

In my book on black men, mothers and grandmothers emerged as the "heroines" through the story's main focus, which was to keep their children safe from the streets where, in an instant, death can, and does, occur. The women's anxiety becomes real when their children become a statistic on a police blotter or a victim of a crime. Many youth in the inner city do not see beyond their neighborhood circumstance and lose hope for an opportunity of a better life. According to C. West (1994, p. 20), there is a "profound sense of psychological depression, personal worthlessness, and social despair." These feelings are true today; societal circumstances remain the same as in the 1990s.

A. Lourdes (1978), in a verse entitled, "A Litany for Survival," captures the essence of black mothers' feelings when she expresses that verbalizing fears is of no benefit; the words are not listened to. The silence remains, and the fears linger: "we are silent [but] we ... are still afraid" (p. 32).

HISTORICAL AND CULTURAL PERSPECTIVE

A Poignant Theme Emerges Early On: The Black Woman Is Alone, Vulnerable, and without a Country

In examining the history of blacks in America, we find an ominous environment. The following oration captures the gist of the African's initial immersion into American society. In 1862, an address was delivered by Sarah P. Redmond in London, beseeching moral support for the enslaved. As later recorded in the *Journal of Negro History* (1942), these anguished words reflect the condition of the African race in America:

> A sad, sad hour for the African race . . . the arrival of the negroes gave new vitality to the enfeebled colony at Virginia, and revived the sinking colonists. The negroes were received as a farmer receives a useful and profitable animal; although, at that time, their services were invaluable. In return for their services, they and their posterity have been doomed to a life of slavery. Then took root chattel slavery, which has produced such physical, mental, and moral degradation upon an unprotected and unoffending race . . . the usual estimate is about four and a half millions . . . in the Southern states. . . . Thousands among the commercial, manufacturing, and working classes, on both sides of the Atlantic, are dependent upon cotton for all material prosperity; but the slaves who have produced two-thirds of the cotton do not own themselves; their nominal wives and their children may at any moment be sold. I call them nominal *wives*, because there is no such thing as legal marriage permitted either by custom or law. (216–18)

The black slave woman's life in America began when she was purchased and included as part of the chattel on the plantation. Oftentimes, she was abused—not only flogged but sexually assaulted. Many times this sexual exploitation would result in her becoming pregnant with the master's child; however, the child was never her own. The child could, and often would, be sold like a commodity to another master on another plantation or added to the master's enslaved workers on his own plantation.

Beaulieu (1999) stated that a "slave woman's body was frequently colonized by the white master" (p. 11) to satisfy his sexual appetite; Beaulieu discusses the fact that slave women were looked at as genderless and placed in the category of "breeder"; they were not "mothers" with an emotional connection to their children. On a figurative and literal level, *breeder* relates to livestock.

Christian (1985) states: "Slave women and men were denied their natural right to the children. . . . Women were valued not for themselves, but for the capacity to breed, that is, to 'produce' workers, and for their ability to nurture them until they were able to work on the plantation" (221). The master made decisions based on economics. If a slave woman was pregnant, the master would, in order to protect his own chattel, lighten her chores partially: "For instance, depending on their stage of pregnancy, pregnant women were considered half or quarter hands" (White, 1999, p. 121).

The masters would manipulate the slave woman. For example, she would be given incentives to get pregnant: "On the birth of a child certain additions of clothing and an additional weekly ration are bestowed on the family, and these matters, as small as they may seem, act as powerful inducements" (White, p. 100). During the period of slavery, the black woman's role as breeder became important because each birth meant an increase in prospective slave hands. Unexpectedly, an interesting sphere of influence emerged. The slave woman gained preeminence over the male slave, or as Oakes (1990) explained, she had a "bargaining chip" that the male slave did not have. She not only did the field work equal to any male slave, but she also multiplied the labor force.

Perhaps it was no mere coincidence that black enslaved women had no status in America. In her research on black women, hooks (1992) reported that the manner in which black women were treated in Africa astounded the eighteenth- and nineteenth-century missionaries; she was submissive, obedient, and in servitude to the black man:

> The poor women of Africa . . . have all the hard work to do. They have to cut and carry all the wood, carry all the water on their heads, and plant all the rice. . . .
>
> You will often see a great, big man walking ahead with nothing in his hand but a cutlass (as they always carry that or a spear), and a woman, his wife, coming on behind with a great big child on her back, and a load on her head. No matter how tired she is, her lord would not think of bringing her a jar of water, to cook his supper with, or of beating the rice, no, she must do that. (p. 17)

As seen by the white slaver, this indoctrination would make her "an ideal subject for slavery" (hooks, 1992, p. 17). This prediction became a reality. On the southern plantation, black women were placed in the same role—submissive, obedient, and in servitude.

In addition, first-generation male slaves who had had prominent roles in their African communities, transplanted their attitudes and behavior to the plantation. For example, one such slave

> had been a priest in his own nation and had never been taught to do any kind of labor being supported by the contributions of the publick; . . . [On the plantation, he] was compelled by the overseer to work, with the

other hands, in the field, but as soon as he had come into his cabin, he took his seat and refused to give his wife the least assistance in doing anything. . . . It appeared that this woman's constitution was broken by hardships, and sufferings, and that she could not live long in her present mode of existence. . . . The overseer refused to protect her, on the ground that he never interfered in the family quarrels of the black people. (Redmond, 1942, p. 235)

From the very beginning, the black slave woman was alone and victimized, but outwardly she showed the strength and conviction to protect her children and to survive. Unfortunately, this same strength left a legacy implying that black women were the "mules" of society—that they could withstand any burden, physical or emotional. This legacy haunts black women today.

Antagonistic relationships between the female slave and the mistress of the plantation were common. Fox-Genovese (1988) wrote that because of the sexual trysts between master and slave, the mistress of the plantation would more often than not be hostile toward the slave woman and her acts of revenge would often result in brutality and murder. In many cases, the slaveholding mistress became more racist than the slaveholding master.

Jones (1985) recorded that because of her own frustrations, the mistress of a plantation would lash out in rage against a slave woman. The mistress's job was to manage the multitude of house slaves, who, more often than not, would be unmanageable. Some also had to deal with an unfaithful and arrogant husband. In such cases, her frustrations led to vicious attacks on the slave woman, particularly in the house, where the mistress had access to a butcher knife or scalding water. Her rash emotional outbursts could result in the enslaved woman being scarred or disfigured for life.

In the *Journal of Negro History* (April 1930), E. Franklin Frazier noted an account of a mistress's strategy to foil her husband's fraternization with a slave woman:

Mistress told sister that she had best get married, and that if she would, she would give her a wedding. . . . Mistress returned delighted from the wedding, for she thought she had accomplished a great piece of work. But the whole affair only enraged her unfeeling husband. . . . [He] determined to be revenged . . . [and] he again cruelly whipped my sister. A continued repetition of these things finally killed our Mistress, who, the doctor said, died of a broken heart. (p. 221)

Evidently, conflicts on the plantation were multidimensional. Hymowitz and Weissman (1978) report remarks by Mary Boykin Chestnut, an upper-class woman from the South, who testified to the hostility:

Like the patriarchs of old, our men live all in one house with their wives and their concubines; and the mulattoes one sees in every family partly resemble the white children. Any lady is ready to tell you who is the father of the mulatto children in everybody's household but her own. Those, she seems to think, drop from clouds. My disgust is sometimes boiling over. Thank God for my country women, alas for the men. (p. 61)

The *Silence* of White Women

Instead of condemning the white man for acts of sexual aggression, it was rumored within the southern white community that black women were "loose" and had a different sense of morality from white women.

White women were helpless against the transgressions of their husbands, but they remained silent. Chestnut wrote about their silence: the plantation wives felt rejected and humiliated; however, they accepted the husband's relationship with the slave women in exchange for his outward "chivalrous veneration" of the wife. This show of adoration allayed the wife's anxiety and fulfilled her need to be valued (Hymowitz and Weissman, 1978, p. 62).

Therefore, to assuage his guilt, the white master placed the southern white women on a pedestal, as the personification of "purity." This model of white southern womanhood was Eurocentric and Victorian in nature. The southern lady was honor bound to further the ideals of character, piety, and elegance.

Fox-Genovese describes the white Southern woman in accordance with Margaret Mitchell's novel, *Gone with the Wind*: "the southern lady was quintessentially milky-white of skin, slow of speech, and innocent of hunger, temper, or passion" (1988, p. 197). In truth, however, these women faced a dilemma that they had no power to resolve.

While the upper-class southern white woman in eighteenth- and nineteenth-century America was accepted as an ideal to emulate, the black woman was accepted as the worker, "society's mule." This derision has resulted in the black woman's feelings of never being beautiful enough. The imagery of white (virtue) and black (impurity) has been institutionalized in literature throughout the ages.

The Helplessness of the Enslaved against the Institution of Slavery: Emotional and Physical Assaults

Although work in the field was arduous and field workers had no status among the domestic slaves (DuBois, 1969 [1908]), it sometimes turned out to be a more suitable arrangement for the enslaved woman. The overseers were brutal in their demands for production, but, to her advantage, she was not observed as closely as in the house. When the woman worked in the field, she was in closer contact to her own children, and she was not on call at all hours of the day and night.

Blassingame (1979) documents the sufferings of Lewis Clarke, a house slave, in a passage from his *Narratives* (1859):

> We were constantly exposed to the whims and passions of every member of the family; from the least to the greatest their anger was wreaked upon us. Nor was our life an easy one, in the hours of our toil or in the amount of labor performed. We were always required to set up until all the family had retired, then we must be up at early dawn in summer, and before day in winter. (p. 251)

The master had the power to control every aspect of a slave's life, such as freedom of movement, "marriage," and the personal relationships of husbands, wives, and children. Even though a master might give his approval for a slave couple to enter into a ceremony of "marriage," the slave couple had no protection under the law and the slave master had absolute control and authority; his power remained sovereign. The master could enter the woman's cabin and rape her; he could sell a member of the slave family to another plantation, permanently separating husband and wife or child and parent. It was an inhumane system, and the central principle was based on the acquisition of wealth and sexual exploitation of the slave woman. In fact, one can say that the plantation system grew into a harem for the white man in the New World. For some masters, the power itself became the point.

In a chapter entitled, "Outsiders," Oakes (1990) states:

> Through the ostentatious display of the master's power and the slave's subordination such episodes transcended their immediate rationale. They captured much of the essence of slavery: the violence, the sexual abuse, and the dishonoring of the slaves through the explicit disregard for their kinship relations. Parents were denied the power to protect their children. Spouses watched helplessly as their mates were brutalized. The slaves were not simply punished for their putative transgressions, they were humiliated and dishonored besides. (p. 21)

White recorded that one of the most horrific times for the male slave was when his wife and children were whipped or raped. If the male slaves wreaked havoc or revenge, the overseer or master would beat them lifeless. Therefore, an act of revenge would be an act of suicide: "Only the uncommon bondsman mustered suicidal courage and took revenge on the white man who had whipped or raped his wife. More common, according to Linda Brent [1973 (1861)], was the man who slipped away and feigned ignorance of the attacks on his wife" (p. 146).

In another recorded incident, published in *Reminiscences of Levi Coffin* (1876), the author wrote about Margaret Garner, a fugitive slave from Kentucky, who killed one of her children rather than have her grow up in a life of slavery. Garner fled from slavery with her children, but, upon being surrounded by fugitive slave hunters, she "seized a butcher knife that lay on the table and with one stroke cut the throat of her little daughter" (quoted in Mintz, 1996, p. 155). This theme emerges in Toni Morrison's *Beloved* (1987), in the genre of the neo-slave narrative, as a statement of conviction and strength and of the choice to be free.

Fox-Genovese (1988) remarked: "The system endowed master with a power that few could defy and the law could barely check. A slave woman, in resisting her condition, risked assaults on her person, the gradual erosion of ties to her [plantation] community, and ultimately, isolation or death" (pp. 395–396). From Henry Bibb's autobiography (1849), Blassingame (1979) reports that: "a poor slave's wife can never be . . . true to her husband contrary to the will of her master. She can neither be pure nor virtuous, contrary to the will of her master. . . . The [slave] woman faced him [the master] alone. She looked on naked power" (pp. 173, 374). Fox-Genovese (1988) confirms: "So long as the power persisted, the slave woman lived always on the edge of an abyss, always confronted a dangerous world in which her naked identity would challenge his in solitary combat" (p. 396).

The Disparity in the System

The state did exercise some control, however minimal. In court cases, jurists weighed the political effects of their decisions:

> Every new law regulating slave behavior was . . . a status report on the balance of power between masters and slaves in the Old South. . . . Slaves were tried for theft and robbery, assault, rape, and murder—all of which raised special problems precisely because the persons involved were not supposed to have "legal personalities" to begin with. (Oakes, 1990, p. 163)

Blassingame states, "By the 1840s ministers and layman had begun suggesting the passage of laws prohibiting the separation of slave families" (1979, p. 174). Nineteenth-century southern ministers were in accord on this issue. They appealed "to the conscience of masters to ensure the inviolability of slave marriages" (p. 174). But the slave master did not find "divine" biblical assertions more convincing than profit and loss.

Blassingame (1979) also records that the treatment of slaves included making them act deferential. He quotes the Rev. Jermain W. Loguen, whose writing was published in *The Rev. J. W. Loguen as a Slave and as a Free Man* (1859):

the slaves were always obliged to approach the door of the mansion, in the most humble and supplicating manner, with our hats in our hands, and the most subdued and beseeching language in our mouths . . . taught to cower beneath the white man's frown, and bow at his bidding, or suffer all the rigor of the slave laws. (p. 257)

It was not uncommon for the children of the master to whip a slave, thereby establishing in white children their sense of superiority over slaves.

The black preacher in the southern plantation, who was also a slave, preached obsequious behavior. He emphasized obedience: "the path of duty is always the path of safety . . . make yourselves, and all around you, as contented and happy as possible where you are" (Blassingame, 1979, p. 132). In this way, the black preacher would gain rewards of money, relief from toil, and sometimes manumission from the master.

The Enslaved Mother and Her Sense of Responsibility

Woodson (1916), the historian and editor of the *Journal of Negro History,* wrote an article chapter titled, *Eighteenth Century Slave Advertisements,* recording numerous accounts of runaway slaves. White (1999) posited that a male slave who was "married" and had children could more freely escape from bondage; he would feel secure that his mate would not abandon the children. The female slave was more likely to stay in servitude rather than take children into the unknown. By the number of advertisements seeking fugitive slaves, it becomes apparent that the greater percentage of fugitives were men. For example, in the 1730s in colonial South Carolina, a full 77 percent of the fugitives were men. Similar statistics existed throughout the South.

For a female slave attempting to escape with her children, the experience was harrowing one. White (1999) states that although in the novel *Uncle Tom's Cabin*, Harriet Beecher Stowe's account of Eliza and her child is fictionalized, the story is true to the historical facts of the plight of many slave women.

Regardless of the fact that the slave woman shared the physical toil in the field on an equal basis with the male slave, additional chores carried into the night. She would take responsibility for her children; she would bring them scraps of food that she had accumulated during the day. Throughout the literature of the slave period, the word "nurture" is used to describe the manner in which the slave woman devotedly took care of her children.

The concept of devoted nurturing on the part of the mother and grandmother also emerged in my study, *Success Factors* (1998), as a necessary survival factor for children growing up in the inner city. It remains the glue that bonds the family.

Woodson gave credence to the idea that the mother's greatest concern was to keep her children from being sold away from her in the many slave advertisements that he compiled and recorded, examining the sale of a female slave and her children: "A Wench, complete cook, washer and ironer, and her four children—a Boy 12, another 9, a Girl 5, that sews; and a Girl about 4 years old. Another family—a Wench, complete washer and ironer, and her Daughter, 14 years old, accustomed to the house" (April 1916, p. 234). In an analysis of the era of slavery, E. Franklin Frazier (1940), attests that his research of slave documents also demonstrated that mothers were the dominant figures within the slave family system.

The Enslaved Father

As many findings reveal, the fact that "The father escaped from slavery or was seen seldom or not at all is sufficient evidence of the mother's place. The father was the visitor, often to the home presided over by the mother" (236). It was impossible to have stability within the slave family. In this way, the master "stole" the manhood of the African male. He provided "the cabin, clothes, and the minimal food for his wife and children. Under such a regime slave fathers often had little or no authority" (Blassingame, 1979, p. 172). In addition, in all of the data reviewed, accounts of white males' sexual advances toward the black slave women were in evidence. As previously inferred, relations within the slave family, and the master's household, were complex and strained.

A Foreshadowing of the Future: Black Women and Black Men

In discussing the relationship between enslaved men and women, White (1999) notes that

> The nature of plantation life required that married relationships allow slave women a large degree of autonomy. . . . In almost all societies where men consistently dominate women, their control is based on male ownership and distribution of property and/or control of certain culturally valued subsistence goods. The absence of such mechanisms in slave society probably contributed to female slave independence from slave men. (p. 153)

As the decades passed and generations of children were born, family ties became the strength for survival in the system. Although the master continued his tight hold on all slaves, usurping every dominion of a slave's life, the slave family would meet in secret to plan acts of resistance:

> Pushed too hard by an overseer, whipped once too often by a master, a field hand's decision to strike back or not was most often made in consultation with family members and in consideration of family attachments. . . . Acts of resistance were often provoked by the master's abuse of a slave's spouse or child, or by a particularly galling intrusion into the slaves' personal affairs. (Oakes, 1990, p. 147)

Eventually, two classes of slaves emerged: a class of mulattoes, produced by sexual relations between the master and slave woman, and a class of field hands. The mulattoes generally became house servants and grew up in close proximity to the white family. They "acquired a conception of themselves that raised them above the black field hands" (Oakes, 1990, p. 258). Eventually, "through emancipation or the purchase of their freedom [mulattoes] became a part of the free class where an institutional form of the Negro family first took root" (p. 258). Because of their lighter color, they were more accepted by the white ruling class.

However, "In the case of field hands who were cut off from contacts with whites and those slaves who were carried along as mere utilities in the advance of the plantation system, family relations became completely demoralized" (Frazier, 1930).

Postslavery Era from 1865

Throughout the generations and beyond 1865, the Negro woman remained steadfast in her responsibility toward her children. Frazier (1966 [1939]) confirms that, by this time, the Negro woman was so conditioned to be the dependable member of the family that she remained spiritually free and totally self-sufficient, qualities slavery had ingrained in her. She did not have to fight for her freedom as white women did—in mind and body. She was on a different page in the woman's struggle; she was not dominated by an outside force; she was the prime mover; she was self-directed. She "owned" herself. By this time, the only fight she had in common with the white woman was over the concept of respect.

In assessing the Antebellum period in American history, Franklin (1969) discusses the Freedmen's Bureau as one of the significant agencies that helped Blacks in the transitional period from slavery to freedom in a political climate that was hostile to them. However, because the Freedmen's Bureau had federal jurisdiction, white southerners were wary that this kind of encroachment might be a maneuver to give Blacks the vote. Nevertheless, the bureau's efforts were vital in aiding the freedmen to relocate, in supervising working conditions, and in helping to establish educational institutions. During Reconstruction, the two main sources of relief for freedmen were the bureau and the black church.

From Farms to Factories

In search of a better life, multitudes of blacks moved northward to escape farm labor reminiscent of plantation life. Unknown to them, the North was experiencing a rapid transition in employment opportunities, from the need for craftsmen to the need for factory workers. Industrialization was rapidly becoming a major factor in urban America. This changing economic circumstance created a crisis for artisans; they were laid off, and assembly line workers were hired.

As a result, the influx of blacks, who were willing to work for lower wages, threatened the existing labor force, and tensions between white and black workers became explosive. In examining the era, Franklin (1969) observed that the impoverished conditions of blacks persisted. Although they had a measure of hope for a better life in the move from South to North, their expectations were never realized: America was not the "melting pot" envisioned by sociologists. On the contrary, practices in the mainstream gave birth to a caste and class system for the African American.

From Past to Present

Omalade (1994) summarized the condition of black women after slavery ended. She said the black men attempted to resurrect their manhood by establishing a patriarchal community with the women as their "wards." The attempt did not work, however. The problem was two-pronged: the black male had difficulty finding long-term employment and the women would never let themselves be "owned" again (p. 15).

With or without their male counterparts, the black woman kept up the good fight for herself and her children. Her past struggle remained an indelible part of her present: yet, she had the indomitable ability to survive, to take care of her children under extreme hardship, and to bear her pain in silence.

Hull (1982) emphasizes that: "women's adaptability to their harsh reality does not give enough attention to the sheer *pain* of living lives with few options" (p. 96). But the importance of these themes became convoluted: when focusing on the black family, researchers concluded that the woman *intentionally* usurped the position of the black man and blamed her for his decline.

In the 1940s and 1950s, the strong but deleterious effects of female-headed households surfaced in the research of historians and sociologists. E. Franklin Frazier's study, *The Negro Family in the United States* (1966 [1939]) discussed the strengths of the black mother, who had to provide for her children under egregious circumstances: extreme poverty, poor housing conditions, and desertion.

But the truth lay within the context of a racist society. The family's plight was caused by the man's inability to obtain decently paying work. Ironically, the black woman's resolve to surmount extreme obstacles was interpreted by many to mean that she was more powerful than the black man—in other words, too powerful—and that she robbed the man of his role in the family and in society. The public awareness of the black family's predicament caused the black male to lose whatever pride he had left. The societal exposure not only humiliated him but also created a further schism between him and the black woman. The black man, once again, felt he was not needed at home.

When the Moynihan Report (*The Negro Family*, 1965) was published, it was sympathetic to black families and called for national action to aid them. But acute phrases such as "the family structure of lower class Negroes is highly unstable . . . and is approaching complete breakdown" and the family structure is "matriarchal" and entrenched in a "tangle of pathology" aroused the ire of black leaders and white liberals. These powerful statements became rallying issues for critics, who rebuked Moynihan's statements as racist.

The report became a landmark study that added to the anguish of the black woman and increased the bias against her. Jones (1985) concluded that the mother's dominant role in the family emasculated young black males, who needed men to emulate, not women. This negative interpretation spun out of control and set off a chain of events that led to further conflicts between the black male and the black female—conflicts that endure.

Angela Davis (1995) attempted to set the record straight. She stated that the woman's role in the slave community was central to the survival of herself, her family, and her race. It was not a position that she elected to serve in, but a condition of slavery that she was drawn into by virtue of her gender, specifically the ability to bear children.

Davis further said that the myth of the "female castrator" creates a divide between black men and black women:

> The matriarch concept . . . is an open weapon of ideological warfare. Black men and women alike remain its potential victims—men unconsciously lunging at the woman, equating her with the myth; women sinking back into the shadows, lest an aggressive posture resurrect the myth in themselves. . . . The myth must be consciously repudiated as myth, and the black woman in her true historical contours must be resurrected . . . a legacy wrought in blood by our mothers in chains. (p. 216)

To state that a black woman's role in the family has resulted in a "tangle of pathology" does not fit the true circumstances. The woman's fortitude emerged from the context; black males were not accepted into America's mainstream culture. As Ralph Ellison (1952) experienced and wrote: they were "invisible." The black woman had to contend with having no one to support her financially or emotionally. The circumstances resulted in women turning to women, in kinship. The black woman's strength came out of necessity.

As my research on young black males show (1998), sons are strongly bonded to their mothers and grandmothers; the bond keeps the young men "on track." In the sons' hearts, their mothers' and grandmothers' stoicism can only be designated as "noble" and "heroic."

Society's discrimination against black men in employment created the woman's desire to forge her way alone, if necessary. Hull et al. (1982) record the dilemma of the black woman, both yesterday and today: "Black women have not been praised by dominant-culture sociologists for their strong role in aiding family stability; on the contrary, they have been strongly criticized" (95).

White America's discrimination against black men and their resulting inability to obtain gainful employment resulted in the need for black women to work, although their men wanted them to stay at home, historically and currently.

Following the negative connotation related to the black woman as being "too powerful," Hymowitz and Weissman (1978) documented statements made by women who, at the time, were the scapegoats:

> about the black matriarchy saying that black women ran the community. Which is bull. We don't run no community. We went out and worked because they wouldn't give our men jobs. . . . There is neither power nor satisfaction in such a matriarchy. There is only bitter knowledge that one is a victim. (p. 337)

Hymowitz and Weissman followed up their observations with a discussion of the results of racism on the black woman, man, and family:

> White society systematically denied black men access to jobs that would allow them to support their wives and children. In this way black men were denied a feeling of manhood, and black women were denied the opportunity to rely on their men. Both sexes often felt disappointed in themselves and each other. (pp. 337–338)

The ripple effect of unemployment on the black man, the resultant loss of self-respect, and the eventual development of the Aid to Dependent Children program (if the man was not living at home) broke apart families. The root cause was blamed on women, not society's racism. The woman was discredited. She was blamed for "emasculating" the man. On the one hand, the woman was perceived as nurturing; on the other hand, she was perceived as a "destroyer." The end result was that she was a "man-loser" and alone (Hymowitz and Weissman, 1978, p. 339).

The *Silent* Accord

Oftentimes, men's inner rage against the system burst into "abusive and brutal [behavior] toward their wives and children" (Omalade, 1994, p. 34). However, many times, women made the decision to "stay at their side in spite of abuse and fear" (p. 89) and maintain silence so as not to authenticate "society's negative stereotyping and treatment of black men" (p. 90). But, more often than not, the woman chose to live alone and become a single parent. Omalade states that researchers do not include in their studies a significant reality: "While social scientists ponder the reasons for so many single mothers, cycles of violence and abuse which rip apart Black couples go unnoticed" (p. 90).

Omalade (1994) also states that, historically, black scholars in institutions of higher education turned away from studying black women and their struggles. Professors trained their students to study conventional scholarship, which is Anglo-centered and objective and detaches researchers from their own voice. If they studied black culture at all, they placed the black man on center stage, looked at black culture from a male perspective, and placed black women in a subordinate position.

Omalade (1994) questions: "Could that be why Zora Neale Hurston died a forgotten woman in an unmarked grave? Or why it took Spelman College, a Black female institution of higher learning, over a century to develop a Black women's center for research and study?" (p. 109). This type of silent accord by black women emerged during the 1940s, at the onset of the civil rights movements, and the 1960s, during the black power movement. The women became the supportive entity and adhesive that held the movements together, including creating organizations. However, when it came to the administrative hierarchy within the organizations, the men appropriated the lead roles and the women took a step back.

The black man's attitude was expressed by Angela Davis, a scholar and political activist of the 1960s:

> I ran headlong into a situation which was to become a constant problem in my political life. I was criticized very heavily, especially by male members of [Ron] Karenga's [U.S.] organization, for doing a "man's job." Women should not play leadership roles, they insisted. A woman was to "inspire" her man and educate his children. The irony of their complaint was that much of what I was doing had fallen to me by default. (quoted in Robnett, 1997, p. 183)

Omalade (1994) speaks of the silence:

> The African woman had been baptised. Since the beginning of time, the power of women came through her. The lives of men and of women were

seen through her eyes. She sang and danced their story. But then she
was raped and became chattel and then she became *silent*. . . . Black
women poets and writers heard all of them and combined their *voices*
into books and poetry. Black women fought against the *silencing*. A few
tried to tell the history and moved toward being a "griot" while remem-
bering the river where the first African woman had been baptised long
before the horror of her sentence of *silence*. (p. 105)

When her power dissipated, only the emptiness of her silence remained. The
themes of black women's silence and strength permeate this study.

Black Women and Community

Black women's strength derives from each other: women nurturing women,
women involved in church activities, and women collaborating in black
women's organizations. These supportive agencies became significant for
building extended kinship relationships, self-esteem, unified principles, and
resilience. The formation of women's organizations was discussed as early as
the 1890s (White, 1999).

In 1896, one of the first organizations was formed: the National Association
of Colored Women. The rallying creed centered on self-help, obtaining decent
jobs, raising the quality of life for women and children, and aiding rural southern black women in their adjustment to urban life in the North. White states
that the safety within black women's affiliations prompted women to speak
openly amongst themselves on many issues: "issues about sexual identity,
struggles with poverty, abuse, self-hatred, and misogyny"(1999, p. 156).

The most sacred institution in the black family's life is the black church.
In my previous study on black males (1998), fifteen of the seventeen students
I interviewed emphasized their religious-spiritual orientation, as reinforced
throughout their lives by their mother, grandmother, or both (Ross, 1998, p.
41). In my present study on women, the findings are similar.

Historically, the religious-spiritual aspect of the black family's existence
is a lifeline for survival. Wade-Gayles (1995) assembled an anthology of
women's voices, titled *My Soul Is a Witness: African American Women's
Spirituality*. Through these writings, she traces the spirituality of African
American women from slavery to the present. She documents how the fundamental truths of existence were recanted in spirituals, how they were used as
a tool for communication, and how they led slaves in the direction of freedom.
The most significant connection of the past to the present is the continuity of
the spiritual. An excerpt from the writing of Katie Geneva Cannon (1995)
reinforces the cultural connections:

In spite of every form of institutional constraint, Afro-American slaves
were able to create another "world," a counterculture within the white-

defined world, complete with their own folklore, spirituals, and religious practices. These tales, songs, and prayers are the most distinctive
cultural windows through which I was taught to see the nature and range
of Black people's response to the dehumanizing pressures of slavery
and plantation life. (p. 21)

The ability to transmit knowledge through the oral tradition of ancient
cultures is a link in the chain from Africa to America.

3

Neo-Slave Narrative

This chapter reviews the genre of the neo-slave narrative and the responses to the literature by Florida Memorial College students in a class on women writers. Black writers today have come full circle in the discovery of who they are—their historical, cultural, and psychological ties to the past. Blurring descriptions of characters and plot lines, they record their collective experiences in the neo-slave narrative and expose the pain and isolation that remain.

Beaulieu (1999) states that the psychological effects of slavery still linger. She supports her views by discussing the novel *Beloved,* written by Toni Morrison (1987). In *Beloved*, the fulfillment of a child's potential and a mother's sense of being and wholeness are lost to humanity forever. Morrison paints a picture of the haunting sense of loss and guilt of an enslaved woman who murders her female child rather than have her experience the inhumanity of slavery. This act of murder is a historical reality, based on a true event— Margaret Garner's act of resistance to slavery in 1851. The slave mother is, in fact, using the only power that she has—obliterating her own existence. Because the delineation of mother and child is not clearly evidenced in Morrison's descriptions, the blurred connection of mother and child creates an image of oneness, representing the unbreakable bond formed in prenatal life, the "impossibility of separating what belongs to the one body from what belongs to the other when the two are joined by the nipple or, rather, by the milk that flows between them, blurring borders. . . . Nursing serves as a figure for the totality and exclusivity of mother-daughter fusion" (61). Ghostly images of the past surface in the neo-slave narrative, bringing past sufferings into the twentieth-century connecting black women to their embittered roots in America. Nevertheless, these stories grounded in the past give the twentieth century African American woman the collective consciousness to surmount their obstacles and to endure.

Trudier Harris remarked, subsequent to the Swedish Academy's selection of Morrison for the Nobel Prize:

> Morrison has written a national epic with a twist firmly rooting black people in the polluted American soil of their slave heritage and transforming that soil to a garden of possibility through the tremendous force of the human will to survive and to thrive. She has thereby reclaimed America for the best of itself. (quoted in Beaulieu, 1999, p. 58)

The contemporary writer renewing the slave narrative feels comfortable with clouding the lines of fiction and reality. It would not be difficult to believe, as Morrison's book suggests, that ghostly apparitions are spiritual elements in the environment that persist throughout time.

Wade-Gayles (1991), in an essay entitled, "Connected to Mama's Spirit," explains that her mother's psychic energy, in life and in death, is part of her African legacy and that her mother's admonishment not to "lock out the spirit" has become a valuable tool for her own survival (p. 215).

Another example is *Jubilee* (1966), a "fuzzy" historical novel, in which A. Walker interrelates the story of her family's history with the epic tale of slavery. In reconstituting and reiterating the role of the nineteenth-century black woman in America, contemporary black women affirm and convey the collective determination, hope, and inspiration that are legendary in the black community (pp. 137–57).

The slave narratives have a direct relationship to the past. Many writers blend the supernatural legacy of Africa into the plot lines of their novels in an attempt to understand their own conflicts—that turbulent legacy that permeates their souls. For example, the forces of nature can be strongly felt in Morrison's *Beloved* (1987) and Gloria Naylor's *Mama Day* (1993).

For the black woman writer, recalling the past is a search for identity, a restructuring of self, and a form of catharsis. Allan (1999) asserts that "black women's narratives now lend an awesome presence to the American literary landscape, smothering the anxiety of displacement that marked their painful gestation" (p. 435).

In reviving slave history through the neo-slave narrative, these writers are reliving the role of their foremothers and preserving the past. The strain that emerges is the brutality of the slave system and the sorrow of the past, which is still working itself out in the present. Enslaved women are the unsung heroines. J. M. Braxton, in an essay entitled, "Ancestral Presence: The Outraged Mother Figure in Contemporary Afra-American Writing" (1999), emphasized that the "violated woman should be recognized as the archetypal counterpart to the male hero" and that "female slave narrators like 'Linda

Brent' should be given the credit for planting the seed of contemporary Black feminist and 'womanist' fiction early in Black American literary tradition" (p. 9).

In historical perspective, the black woman should be credited, not only for uplifting her race, but also for discussing the politics of gender; she was immersed in racial and gender exploitation, and she was aware of both, as documented in the oral testimony of Sojourner Truth in 1852:

> there is a great stir about colored men getting their rights, but not a word about the colored woman; and if colored men get their rights, and not colored women theirs, you see the colored men will be masters over the women, and it will be just as it was before (quoted in hooks, 1992, 4).

Also relevant is Anna Cooper's statement in *A Voice from the South* (1988 [1892]): "The white woman could at least plead for her own emancipation; the black woman, doubly enslaved, could but suffer and struggle and be *silent*. She is confronted by both a woman question and a race problem" (134, italics added). In looking at the past and its reflections on the present, Alice Walker writes in *In Search of Our Mothers' Garden* (Gates, 1997): "Guided by my heritage of a love of beauty and a respect for strength—in search of my mother's garden, I found my own" (p. 2387).

STUDENT RESPONSES TO THE READINGS

The importance of black women writers to the young is summed up in an essay written by student Khalia Jelks, who was Miss Florida Memorial College 2000–2001. In a class composition, Khalia summed up the essence of Alice Walker's thoughts and the meaning that she derived from the literature:

> Alice Walker discusses the "muzzled and often mutilated, but vibrant, creative spirit . . . of our mothers, grandmothers, and great-grandmothers." She expresses that black women have always possessed a deep, rich spirituality that has been suppressed. The black woman's search was to find that secret place where women were allowed the opportunity to "feed that creative spirit," and she sought to discover how her spirituality was passed on through the generations. Walker eventually realizes and reveals that ". . . so many of the stories that I write, that we all write, are my mother's stories." She explains that her mother's voice is part of her own creative spirit and that she, too, is able to evoke her spiritual nature in solitude.

Khalia discovers: "In search of her mother's garden, Walker found her own traces of creativity and resilience. 'Whatever rocky soil she landed on, she turned into a garden. . . . she is radiant. . . . She is involved in work her soul must have.' (*Norton Anthology of African American Literature,* p. 2386)." Khalia emphasizes that: "Alice Walker could not fully define her present until she understood her past—the inherited strengths, passions, and creativity from our ancestors—to comprehend our historical identity in order to pass on the meaning of our culture." (2384) Michael Lang, who was an English major, also discussed *In Search of Our Mother's Garden* and the significant meaning that he derived from the literature: "This essay speaks of Black women searching for the creative spirit that was suppressed in their mothers and grandmothers in order to inspire new works. Black women of old were unaware of the richness they held. They were more than mere women, they were Saints" (2380). Michael asserts:

> In the essay, Alice Walker includes a poignant perspective of the South during post-Reconstruction, as expressed by Jean Toomer, in the early twenties: Toomer described Black women as ". . . exquisite butterflies trapped in an evil honey, toiling away their lives in an era, a century, that did not acknowledge them, except as the mules of the world" (p. 2381).
>
> Walker insists that our grandmothers and mothers were not Saints, but Artists. The strain of enduring their unused and unwanted talent drove them insane (p. 2380) (Margaret Garner's act of infanticide attests to this).

Michael asks: "What did it mean for a Black woman to be an artist in this time?" He finds the answer in Walker's assertion: " '. . . to be an artist and a black woman, even today, lowers her status in many respects, rather than raises it, yet artists we will be' (p. 2384). The title, *In Search of Our Mother's Garden,* is 'a personal account that is still shared, in its theme and meaning, by all of us.' " Michael, too, gives affirmation to the creative spirit of black women, yesterday and today,

> "which pops out in wild and unlikely places . . . the muzzled and often mutilated, but vibrant, creative spirit that Black women inherited," and have handed down through the generations. Often [these historic women] wrote and signed their works "Anonymous," because they would be punished if the true author were known. (*Norton Anthology of African American Literature,* 2315–2322)

The blurring of the past and present does emerge: White (1999) discusses the negative self-image that also survives among black women—a complex strain that remains: "There's an in-group racism where light complexions, keen features, straight hair seem to be more desirable. Very dark women speak about being discriminated against by other black women ... we as black women grew up feeling we weren't quite pretty. It's nothing explicitly stated, but something you feel" (p. 244). The consciousness of skin color emerges in the writings of major black literary figures such as Toni Morrison, in *The Bluest Eye;* Paule Marshall, in *Reena,* Maya Angelou, in *I Know Why the Caged Bird Sings*; and Gwendolyn Brooks, in *Maud Martha* (Hull et al., 1982, p. 210). These writings are personal statements that reflect the divided self.

Bridget Gibbs, an English education major, expressed her own observations as an African American woman by analyzing Gwendolyn Brooks's theme of a divided self. In discussing the novel, *Maud Martha,* Bridget says that the story is based in reality, because if an African American woman has dark skin color, she generally comes to regard herself as less attractive than her lighter sisters. In the novel, Maud is repeatedly treated as undesirable by members of her own community, as well as members of other ethnic groups. In this writing, Bridget recognizes the dilemma that black women face, and she, too, broods about the question of color differences that have added to "black women's rage." Bridget's further research leads her to the acute awareness that the novel is an expression of Brooks's own feelings and experiences.

However, Bridget celebrates the direction that Zora Neale Hurston takes to define herself within an emotionally healthy perspective, with "a sense of black people as complete, complex, undiminished human beings." Bridget states that Hurston's writings come from strength: "Her writings are rooted in self-exploration, self-empowerment, and self-liberation. The 'outsider' community does not define her; she looks within and defines herself." In the essay, "How it Feels to be Colored Me," Hurston asserts her strength: "Sometimes, I feel discriminated against, but it does not make me angry. It merely astonishes me. How can anyone deny themselves the pleasure of my company? It is beyond me" (*Norton Literature by Women,* p. 1501) Nevertheless, in an essay entitled "Private Racism," Khalelah Patterson, a Florida Memorial College English major, reflects on the enduring legacy of color and the conflicts that it creates in her:

When thinking about race issues deeply embedded in the American psyche, we often think of the racial tension that exists among blacks and whites. Many African American men can reflect on racial issues that have shaped their struggle. Many can give accounts of being harassed for "driving while black," while others can tell about the position that they didn't receive because of the less qualified white contender.

Khalelah further explains:

It is rare for any African American to speak first and freely about the prejudice they endure from their own people. But I am quite aware of the biases that exist amongst African Americans. Because of my skin tone, there are many incidents that have shaped who I am amongst my people. . . . From my memory, Spike Lee was the first African American to bring to the American public the very real "color" issue in the African American community. What he displayed on the big screen in the movie *School Daze* was something that I was too familiar with. Just as fair-skinned black actresses portrayed the young ladies of the "snobby sorority," those who do not know me use the term "snobby" to describe me. There have been many instances where African Americans have acknowledged my skin tone before they have acknowledged me as a person. Even in a college class setting, I have been used as an example of the slave master and slave product.

I sometimes feel as if I should personally write an "I'm sorry" letter to every African American that is reminded of the rape of their fore-mothers when they set eyes upon my skin. I was once told that I should embrace my white side. I found that amusing, because I do not know of any white family members. The term "Red" has been negatively used to describe me, only making it clear that there is a negative for being "Red." Although I, at times, feel that this struggle is for me alone, I know I am not alone. My darker sisters struggle also. They are discriminated against more than fair-skinned sisters are. Just as the "earthy soror" stated in *School Daze*, she felt like a token for her extra dark skin. I have heard conversations about a person being *so* black as if black skin is a negative. In the media, the representation of dark-skinned women is rare in the sea of Halle Berrys and Vanessa Williamses.

I believe that the need to embrace all shades must happen in the African American community. In order to excel, we must first come together. I am quite aware of my skin, and I am comfortable in the skin I am in. I could only hope that the rest of my community could feel the same way.

The students find their own way through reading, discussing, analyzing, and steering themselves toward the path of education.

4

Herstory: Student Voices and Postreview of the Literature

This chapter capsulizes student responses to interview questions and unfolds "herstory." The emerging findings from the interviews of the women students take a different slant from the findings from the men's interviews. The men emphasized the bonding of mother to child; the nurturing of mother to son; the women reflect on the strength of mothers who never married, the single status of the majority of black women, babies out of wedlock, feelings of desertion by fathers, abuse by men, and neighborhood violence. The following quotations are poignant remarks excerpted from the interviews:

STUDENTS' ASSESSMENT OF MOTHERS' ROLES
AT HOME AND IN THEIR LIVES

My mother is the dominant figure in the home. Whatever she says is the rule. She controls the finances and determines how much we will spend and save.

My mother is a hardworking, strong single parent. She has always taught me how to be a strong woman. I grew up with my mother and she took care of us [five children] by doing the best that she could.

My mother always encouraged us to do better in life than she did. To reach for more and to plan for a better future. The one thing she always instilled in me is the importance of having a good education.

My mom and I didn't talk about sex. We didn't discuss anything like that. But, I remember the one time I asked her about sex, she said, "It didn't feel good, don't do it, and she made a scene like it must not be good. But she was doing it! We didn't discuss it after that scene.

STUDENTS' OBSERVATIONS ON SINGLE MOTHERHOOD

In my short lifetime, I have come in contact with young women who became pregnant on purpose. I feel that they lack love in their lives, and they lack strong parental guidance. They look to a child to give them unconditional love.

In most cases, young pregnant girls follow their mothers' lead, which is single motherhood. Teenage single mothers have no idea how to raise children. These young women think the child will fulfill emotional needs. But, a baby is not a doll—not a toy that you dress up, carry around, show off, then put down. Unless a mother has patience, gives proper guidance, and instills good values, the child does not have a chance in this society.

I had one best friend who got pregnant. I feel that the reason that she got pregnant was for her mother's attention. She said her mother stopped showing her attention, so she dropped out of school in the tenth grade and became a stripper. She told me in that way, she would get attention. Now, she stopped stripping; she is twenty years old and on her third kid. In my opinion, she should have finished her education, but she preferred the other way. To me, that is the way to get "trapped" into a life of poverty.

It is said that your child is the only one who will love you unconditionally. Many young women seek to find that love. These young women want someone to love them so badly that they sacrifice their bodies and their lives for that love. The temptation overpowers their better judgment.

My mother has always been a single parent who has raised us alone from when I was seven years old, and now I am twenty years old. I now realize how hard it is being a single parent; it is always a struggle. My own personal belief is that mothers should never give up on their children. They need to talk to their kids. They should always talk to their kids. Mothers need to be the mother and father when there is no father in the house.

If you do not neglect your kids, they will understand that although they do not have a father they have a loving mother who cares. There are a lot of strong, independent women who are out there doing a good job.

STUDENTS' DEPICTION OF GRANDMOTHERS' ROLES IN THEIR LIVES

My grandmother was the go-between. She never took sides; she was another listening ear. She gave her opinion. She made sure that my mother was raising me without hating my father. She always allowed me to make my own choices; she would give me the pros and cons to each side, but I would make the decision. She was like a counselor or advisor.

When my grandmother found out that I was pregnant [out of wedlock, fifteen years old], she was very hard on me. I was the family's last hope. I disappointed my grandmother, and I think she still hasn't recovered. My grandmother is still very disappointed in me. She probably won't be satisfied until she has my college degree hanging over her bed, then she'll probably feel better.

STUDENTS' LINK TO THE CHURCH

The church creates calm for me like a garden. It is a place where I go to feel like I have a family and to associate myself with people who have had similar experiences. I sympathize with others and learn that I am not the only one in the world who suffers—that suffering is a human condition. I have thought of myself like grass, and my problems like the rain. Problems help to make me grow, and at church, we help each other to get through problems.

The church taught me that it was not good to do sinful acts; it taught me to respect my elders and always be positive. The church also taught me not to be influenced by my peers in a negative way.

My mother and grandmother grew up in the church. It was a generational tradition. It was mandatory that I go to church.

STUDENTS' COMMENTS ON PEER PRESSURE

I see the negative results of peer pressure right now; students follow other students. The girls are fresh out of high school and are out of the house for the first time. The girls are doing wrong, but they don't understand it.

I sometimes tell my roommate to be careful. I tell her that she is going to end up being a single mother with no support from the man, but she makes her own choices.

Some girls get caught up with guys and get pregnant. Some girls belong to a gang and sell drugs. I think it has a lot to do with the environment they are in.

STUDENTS' IMAGE OF FATHERS

My father was in jail from the time I was six years old, and I do not remember him at all. When I became eighteen, I decided that I wanted to meet him, and I drove to the state prison in Georgia. I was just curious, and I wanted to see him. There, I met him. My mother never really told me anything about my father, because she thought it was in my best interest not to know. After I met him [in prison], I kept in touch with him by talking on the telephone a couple of times a week. Eventually, I figured out bits and pieces of his story. My mom gave me some information to read which made me understand what happened. My father did evil things. Now I can see why my mother did not tell me; now I understand. I stopped writing to him, and I do not know if I can ever forgive him. He does not know that I am in school; he does not know that I am in college and concentrating on making a better life for myself than what my mother had.

I give him respect because he is my father, but I don't particularly like him. He does not accept responsibility. I did learn from him what qualities I would like in a man—those qualities would be the opposite of what he showed to me.

I know I lost something important in my life because I never met my father. But I don't really know what I lost. When I see my best friend with her two parents at home, I feel an emptiness. I can actually say that I am jealous. When I was a small child, my father left us; I am the one that suffered. No one took his place. There is no one that I can call "dad." Sometimes I look at faces of black men to see if there is someone out there that I look like.

"The Role of the Absent Father"

To more fully understand a young college student's feelings, I am including Khalelah Patterson's analysis, "The Role of the Absent Father," and a discussion of the effect it has on the African American community. Her critique penetrates into the heart of the issue and gives an insightful commentary of what she sees as the "norm," the strong matriarchal presence. She shares her thoughts about the continuing crisis in African American homes:

In many households this strong matriarchal presence is due to the absence of the father. The absence of the father has become a generational cycle in the African American home. The absence of the father affects the conditions of the African American in America. The role of the African American father is no longer defined within the home. Many fathers have abandoned the responsibility of home and children. The absence of the father leaves the young male in the household wondering what it takes to be a man. Also, the absence of the father leaves the young African American female yearning for the affection of her daddy. These feelings manifest themselves in greater ways that seem to shape the status of the black American. For example, the African American male confuses manhood with exaggerated expressions of aggression. These aggressive acts usually end in violence. This theory may explain why many young males end up dead or in jail.

The black woman is not exempt from the struggle of her man. The absence of her father leads the woman looking for love out of desperation. She wants to right the wrongs of her fatherless childhood. For years, her fatherless mother and grandmother explained to her about men; thus, her perceptions of relating to men become confused. These conditions lead to greater loss of respect and trust within the African American community. Many young men perpetuate the abandonment of their fathers by abandoning their own family. This creates a cycle of single-parent homes with mainly the mother at the helm. This image of the strong mother is very comforting to the young girl who no longer has a healthy relationship with her child's father. If you ask a woman if she can successfully raise a son without a father figure, she will quickly tell you, "Yes." However, if you ask that young man what does he miss, he will say his father. The question they ask is "How can my mom teach me to be tough and essentially to be a man?"

I believe that the African American male needs to be more active in the life of their children. Rearing strong and confident males is the root to saving our community. This is the role of the absent father.

The disturbing trends, if left alone, leave an imprint of hopelessness for the future.

ACTS OF VIOLENCE

Particularly distressing to the students are acts of violence:

People are frustrated and instead of channeling that energy and anger toward positive changes, they just take it out on each other. The violence between black and white communities is obviously from unresolved conflicts. We have lost sight of ourselves as a people.

There is a lot of drug-related violence, black on black crime and gangs. The young guys are out there killing for a little bit of money such as twenty-five dollars.

Kids don't know how to deal with their anger. They take revenge if they have to. I don't think they realize that death is permanent—that when you kill somebody, you just don't end their life, you end your life, too. They have to learn to deal with anger; everything does not require a gun.

Parents are not doing their job. They need to supervise their children. They need to keep the children busy with after-school activities. Girls and boys need interests to occupy their time, otherwise they might fill up their time with negativity, which will lead them into trouble.

Most of the violence that I experience has been in my home. One of my older sisters beat me up all the time. As a result, my vision is messed up, because she used to punch me in my eyes, and I wear glasses now. I saw my father hit my mother; yes, most of the violence that I experienced in my life has been in the home.

I have witnessed one of my close neighbors being shot by a policeman. As he went to pull out his wallet from his pocket to show his identification, he was shot down. My neighbor was not armed. Since that time, I have been afraid of the police. Black people experience a lot of violence [that] comes from the police.

Where I am from, crimes happen every day. Many of my friends who I grew up with, got shot. They were like brothers to me. The crime really scares me and makes me want to get my mother and whole family out of the 'hood. I pursue my dreams even more, no matter how hard it gets. I want a better life.

I have seen drive-by shootings. Guys coming up to other guys with guns, saying that they owe them money. If they do not get what they are asking for, they will shoot. [Those are] the kind of crimes that I have seen.

Mostly young people from ages nineteen to twenty-six are the ones who cause the crime. They get involved in crime because of their need to buy drugs. They also kill people for drug money. This generation is hooked on crack rock [crack cocaine].

I know in the black community a lot of brothers are angry; they have a problem with society, and the police harass them. Some of them just give up. They are not given the same opportunities as other groups of people. They try to make a way for themselves through the "streets." They start looking at each other without value. Some of them, it seems, find it easy to kill people. I don't know where all that anger is coming from, and why they are doing bad things to each other.

My oldest brother was killed by a gunshot to his back. He was coming home from a date. Guys jumped out of the bushes and said, "Nigga, we got you." But they didn't steal any money, so I am not sure why they killed him.

My other brother died; his girlfriend stabbed him in the stomach, and it cut his aorta. He died from internal bleeding.

Rage stems from young people's feelings of alienation, of being an "outsider."

They feel misunderstood and that no one hears them. They have no respect for other people; they have no respect for authority, and they just don't care.

They feel that they don't have anything to lose, because they are so down and *out* right now. It does not really matter to them if they are violent, or if they kill somebody and go to jail right now. Many of the younger ones know they are not going to get the death penalty, because they are not eighteen. They are going to get right back out after a certain period of time.

However, the students who overcome the obstacles in their circumstances demonstrate fortitude, responsibility, and caring.

When I make a decision, I . . . think about whether my mother would be proud of me or not. I . . . consider in my heart if I [am] doing right and if my mother would support my actions. If I don't feel good about the decision, I [will] not get into it.

You should always think about God when making a decision, because he will judge you.

The obstacles to my success would have to be negative feedback. That includes people who do not want to see me succeed and would try to hurt me, as I am trying to advance myself. Because of these negative impacts, I always reevaluate by telling myself that I am going to succeed. I know that I will succeed regardless of who is trying to stand in my way.

I have to overcome my shy ways. I stay by myself a lot. I have to make friends in college. All my friends are home. But I always stay focused on my schoolwork. My ability to get a college education makes me happy. I want to have a better life than my sisters.

Students give serious thought and explicit reasons for their motivation to succeed:

I want to succeed for my unborn kids, and I want to be somebody. To me, being somebody is being the best mom and the best wife in the whole wide world—I want to have a husband who loves me and respects me. I want to have children who are happy—having happy children is like a prize. The strong will that I have inside me motivates me to succeed. I am motivated in my heart. I want to prove that I can do it.

My professors encourage me to express myself in a daily journal and not to keep everything bundled up inside. This leads me to think about my future. I want to succeed in college so that I will be independent.

What motivates me to succeed is the fact that I will be the first one in my immediate family to graduate from college. My sister went to college, but she got pregnant and came home. My mother went to college, but she never graduated. My father only graduated from high school. I would definitely be the first person in my immediate family to graduate from college.

When I was a freshman in college, I got pregnant. But I came back to finish school. Now I have a little girl to think about, so I am back in college so that my child will have a decent future. She motivates me to succeed.

I always thought of achieving my goals. In the past, I wanted to become a successful basketball player; now, I want to get a college degree. I am motivated by my mother. My mother always encouraged me to reach where she did not. She instilled in me the importance of a good education.

The thirst for knowledge motivates me. Success is knowledge. Success is not acquiring tangible things. It is spiritual understanding and self-discovery. Having the motivation to pursue knowledge, gives me hope for a good future, and I want to share what I have learned with others.

STUDENTS' RESPONSES TO GOAL-SETTING

I set out the goal to graduate from high school. I did. I set out the goal to graduate from college. I will graduate in May. I set out to reach and keep my grade point average at three points, and I have been doing that. So far, I have accomplished my goals. I am motivated by each goal that I set, and my actions follow.

Despite everything that I saw out there, I have a positive dream for myself. And I work hard toward my dream.

I want to be a strong self-reliant woman that stands up for what she believes in. I am not going to let anyone discourage me.

STUDENTS' ADVICE TO YOUNG BLACK WOMEN
IN THE COMMUNITY

I recommend that young black women are very selective and observant when selecting a mate, so that their children, especially their young girls, will grow up feeling secure and confident about themselves.

It is important to have a mother for guidance, but without a father, a girl does not really know how to behave in a relationship—what to expect from a man, what to tolerate and what not to tolerate. My advice is to search out for a man that can serve as a role model for your children.

Single parenting is not working. Young women should learn about the hardships. Single motherhood is too accepted in our society. I think mothers accept their daughters' pregnancies, because, they, too, had children without getting married. Their own feelings of guilt prevent them from showing disappointment and anger at their daughters' pregnancies.

My only recommendation is to make goals for yourself. Decide what you want in your future. If you decide that you want a house with a white picket fence, a family, and a dog, then you have to work toward that goal. You can't waste your young adulthood goofing off and doing whatever you think you are big and bad enough to do. It's a matter of preparation; it's very progressive.

I would recommend that young black women stay positive and put God first in all things, to think about the consequences before doing wrong.

My number one recommendation is to get your education. Also, try to have a stable income and stable family life, before bringing any children into the world.

POSTREVIEW OF THE LITERATURE

From the data in the interviews and the statistics of male and female survival rates, the most significant factor that emerges for a better life for the contemporary black woman is the determination to stay in school, obtain a college degree, and pursue professional status.

The success factors of African American women over African American men strongly relate to their constancy and drive to better themselves through education. African American women are upwardly mobile through education: the *Journal of Blacks in Higher Education* (Cross, 1999–2000) reports that "From 1977 to 1995 black women steadily increased their share of all doctorates awarded to African Americans. In 1996 black men appeared to be reversing the trend. But since 1996 black women have made strong gains on black men" (p. 83).

The *Journal of Blacks in Higher Education* (Cross, 2000–2001) addressed the latest trends of enrollment figures in law schools: "Black women now make up 59.6 percent of the African American enrollments at the nation's 50 highest ranked law schools. This is 15 percentage points higher than for women enrollments as a whole" (p. 64).

The same journal (Cross, Summer 2001, p. 33) notes that black women are higher achievers in college than black men and that they are responsible for closing the income gap between whites and blacks, as indicated in the 1999 U.S. Census Bureau statistics.

The *Journal of Blacks in Higher Education* (Cross, Winter 2001–2002) also stated that "in the 1999–2000 academic year, black women earned 23,158 master's degrees compared to 10,408 for black men. Thus, black women accounted for 69 percent of all master's degrees awarded to African Americans. This is up from 63 percent only a decade ago" (p. 102).

The following gender issues are cited for reasons regarding the purposed success of black women compared to black men, in education and in life:

(a) black women have stronger coping skills and motivation than black males;

(b) black women obtain jobs easier than black men; they are not perceived as a threat to white males in the work environment, as are black men;

(c) black women do not feel as discriminated against as black men; black men's strong feelings of being discriminated against produce a "victim mentality," which further curbs their motivation (this particular data has not been proven, but it is, nevertheless, set forth as an explanation);

(d) black women are more readily hired; they fill two minority slots—gender and race;

(e) seventy-five percent of black children spend a significant portion of their childhood without a father in the home, demographers claim, a situation that "sets up" the boy for failure—the male child has no man to emulate or guide him into a meaningful future. (pp. 33–34)

Data collected by the U.S. Census Bureau reveals the percentage of bachelor's degrees by race and gender (cited in Cross, Autumn 2000). In an apparent twenty-two-year trend (1976 to 1997), the information discloses a steady decline in percentages of bachelor's degrees awarded to black men. The question posed in the article was, "Could it possibly be that in 100 years there will be no black men earning a college degree?" The forecast advances the theory that if the downward spiral continues, the conjecture is bleak: black men will be "out of higher education altogether and black women would earn all the bachelor's degrees awarded to African Americans" (p. 124). What does this say about the destiny of young African American women? Is there a future within the security of marriage and family; or should the African American woman plan for a future that may not include a man?

The focus of this study is directed to youth growing up in an inner city environment. The dire circumstances of the inner city influence the critical issues affecting the black male; the resulting issues influence the critical position of the black female.

5

Synthesis: Similarities and Differences between Male and Female Studies

In *Success Factors of Young African American Males at a Historically Black College* (Ross, 1998) and *Success Factors of Young African American Women at a Historically Black College* an intersection of experiences emerges. This chapter discusses similarities and differences between the two studies, strong impressions that emerge, and conclusions on the study on young black women.

Similarity in factors that both male and female students encounter include the following:

1. fatherless homes, economic hardship, and early exposure to violence in inner city neighborhoods;
2. when the father resides in the home, he is described as "passive," the mother is described as "dominant";
3. children see images of mothers out of wedlock, abusive male-female relationships, and poverty;
4. young men raised in the inner city may succumb to drug trafficking, often so that they can obtain money to help put food on the table; young women raised in the inner city often succumb to the role of lookout to protect their men.

However, male and female experiences also differ:

1. the dominant image of the mother or grandmother hovering over the young men is an impression that they feel throughout their lives; the young women, on the other hand, inherit their mother's role—to keep their sons alive and "nurtured";

2. both men and women in the sample demonstrate that they affect their own fate; early on, the perception of danger in the 'hood (neighborhood) causes some young men reared in the inner city to avoid the streets; early on, the awareness that she will likely live without a man causes the young woman to consciously prepare herself to become self-reliant;

3. the young black woman generally finds her way through education; the young black man generally finds his way through sports;

4. in examination of the verbal expressions of the male students, it became apparent that the young men used expressions that connote effort and change, symbolic of "escape" from their confining enclave, the inner city; housing projects were described as prison-like, which "makes me push forward. . . , just touch it, reach, grasp, steer . . . toward the American dream"; in examination of the verbal expressions of the women, it becomes apparent that they describe their circumstances realistically, like a news reporter on the scene.

The role of the woman is of silent observer and protector. However independent she is, she is not free. She remains strong, but she still carries a burden and remains a victim.

Nevertheless, the collective life force in the inner city remains intact. One feels the energy in the metaphoric language of the young men interviewed for *Success Factors of Young African American Males* (1998) as well as in the interviews of the young women in this study (2002).

IMPRESSIONS THAT EMERGE FROM THE INTERVIEWS

In a predominantly white society, situations occur wherein both blacks and whites continue to share in a battle of wits, the same type of survival technique used by master and slave.

One of the major factors for violence in the black community is that young men, if challenged, will not back down. If aggrieved, they will confront the aggressor. In most instances, the young man in the hostile inner city environment has a need to defend his "macho" image—the part of his psyche that is totally his own.

The young girl who gets pregnant in her teenage years feels a lack of love in the home and so turns inward, then outward, for someone to love. She believes that a child will fill the emptiness in her being. While her emotional self is working itself out, she blunders toward an unknown future.

There is no one to guide the young woman into a safe haven. Although her mother may have stressed the importance of being independent of a man, the young woman generally believes that her man will stay committed to her over the years, that their feelings toward each other are unique, and that the child will be an everlasting bond. But when both are poor, having a child out of wedlock locks them into the welfare system (underclass), which they have unwittingly chosen for themselves.

WHAT IS THE REALITY FOR THE WOMAN AND CHILD?

The man generally gives no support, either emotional or financial, and the child may become deeply scarred by the bitterness of her mother and the absence of a male parent. Oftentimes, the man is imprisoned, disappears, or is murdered. While the young man's macho image is reinforced by impregnating the woman, the young woman's momentary sense of joy fades when she is abandoned by the man. Although she may feel that her lost childhood is recovered through her "doll-like" baby, the child grows up quickly and out of her reach. Then, she has another relationship, another child, and the cycle repeats itself.

However, as time yields negative experiences, more often than not, the woman does not want to marry the man who is the father of her child. She will hesitate, assess her situation, and decide that she can pursue a better dream without being encumbered by the plight of the black man. Her life thus becomes a lonely journey.

CONCLUSION

Both studies reveal students' strong ties to family and extended kinship relationships; strong impetus to succeed in college so that their family will be proud of them; and selflessness and cooperative feeling toward helping each other, if the need arises.

The bond and cooperation between individual and family emerges very clearly in my study of young black men (Ross, 1998). While growing up, the young men were emotionally embraced by mothers, grandmothers, sisters, aunts, and fictive kin (close relationships with those not literally related). These attachments were strong survival factors; these attachments are to women.

In the present study of young African American women, they, too, are emotionally embraced by mothers, grandmothers, sisters, aunts, and fictive kin. As with the young men, these attachment remain strong survival factors and are to women.

African American women have come a long way—all by themselves they fought to survive, every step of the way. Today's educated youth, both male and female, are on the same page—both genders have confidence that education can make a difference in their lives and their family's lives.

Students reiterate that racism is not an excuse for failure—that young people have to forge ahead without excuses—that the pursuit of an education leads to positive outcomes for themselves as well as their family, culture, and nation. They are presently maturing into wholeness with confidence.

As shown, *Success Factors of Young African American Males* (Ross, 1998), the young men recognize the important role that their mothers have played in keeping them on the right track; in *Success Factors of Young African American Women*, the young women reveal that they have consciously taken on the traditional role of African American mothers—the role of nurturer, protector, and keeper of the haunting silence of being alone.

Appendix: Selected Interview Transcripts

INTERVIEW 1

Q: What factors do you identify as contributing to your success?
A: I always wanted to be able to succeed. I've always had the urge to want to help people especially in education. God is a big factor in my success. Without my strong desire to help others, and knowing God is part of my life, I wouldn't be able to succeed at all.

Q: Is that your motivating factor?
A: Yes, definitely.

Q: What factors do you identify as obstacles to your success?
A: Peer pressure, peer pressure in high school. Many people said that I couldn't succeed, that I would get pregnant before I went to college, that I would ruin my life—that type of negative feedback was an obstacle, but I now see it as a motivating factor. I had to prove that I could get a college degree to myself first, then let people know that I did accomplish something special.

Q: Who gave you negative feedback?
A: I have family members that said negative comments to me; they did the same to my brother, and their predictions came true. My brother did go to jail. They always told me that I was going to get pregnant, or I would never finish college. I believe they want me to succeed, but they are afraid I will fail, so they think I need to be constantly reminded that I could fall.

Q: What caused your brother's downfall?
A: He was at the wrong place at the wrong time; that's basically what happened. They're trying to pin him with a murder charge. Hopefully he will

not have to wait a year for the trial. That negative stuff always sticks in your head.

Q: Did the negative feelings from family members affect his life?
A: Yes. That was a strong factor. Also, our father was not in our lives. I know that did a lot of damage to him. I was young when my mother and father divorced. I don't really remember him in my life, but he did a lot of damage to my brother. He couldn't really find himself as a man; our father not being in our lives caused a lot of serious problems for my brother.

Q: What was your reaction when your brother was put in jail?
A: I was really hurt. When they called me and told me what happened, I thought they were going to tell me that he was dead, that he was killed. But they told me he went to jail. It really hurt, because I know he's not that type of person; my brother never had a criminal record. He just got married three months before he went to jail; he has a family; he has three boys; it really hurt me, because his sons need him while they are growing up—just like he needed his father. There is nothing I can really do, but just pray for him and hope that the Lord will help us in this situation. He needs to be home for his family.

Q: How old is he now?
A: He's twenty-five.

Q: Do you have other siblings?
A: I have a twenty-eight-year-old stepsister; she's my stepfather's daughter; I have an eleven-year-old adopted brother. I have another brother; we have the same dad, but different moms, he's six months older than me. And I have two stepbrothers and a stepsister from my stepmother. My dad got remarried.

Q: Do you connect with the family?
A: Not really. I don't really feel connected to my stepbrothers and stepsisters, because I didn't grow up with them.

Q: Did your mother support the children? Did she ever get married?
A: My mother, brother, and I lived with my grandmother. She had a house, and thirteen of us lived in her house. We were family; we lived there for a while until my mother got work. My mother got remarried when I was about nine years old, and it was hard for me when she got remarried. I was used to being with my mom and my brother.

Q: Are you speaking about the brother that is now in jail?
A: Yes.

Q: Can you describe the house that you grew up in?
A: It was an older house. There were a lot of us—my grandmother, my mom, her sister, her brother, my cousins' three kids, my other cousin, Shawn; I think there were about thirteen of us living there, and we slept everywhere. I had

two uncles that lived there. We tried to keep the house fixed up the best we could. At that time, we all went to church, and we stuck together as a family.

Q: Who took care of the children?
A: My grandmother. My grandmother took care of us and other children that lived in the neighborhood everyday. My grandmother took care of everybody, everybody in the neighborhood.

Q: At that time, how old was your grandmother?
A: About fifty or sixty years old. She would take care of everybody in the neighborhood. I remember that she told me about a girl that was being chased by a guy that was beating her, and she took the girl and her three children in. Every day a new person was in our house, but my grandmother was never scared. She took care of everybody, everybody.

Q: Do you see your grandmother often?
A: Yes. I still see her very often; I visit her when I go home; she's doing really well.

Q: How does she get her strength?
A: She is like the backbone of our whole family. Everybody in our family can tell you that she's the backbone of our whole family. She helped keep everything together. She prays; she stays on her knees in prayer about any and everything. Whenever anybody needs guidance, they go to her and ask her to pray for them. It is like she has a connection to God; everybody admires her, and they know that she is real.

Q: You mentioned that your peers tried to upset you. What did they do or say?
A: They would try to get me involved with things that they were doing. They would say, "Just try it [marijuana]. It won't hurt, you only live once." I had peer pressure since I was young; they wanted to see me like them. My peers were really rough on me in high school. In my twelfth year, I decided to separate from all of it and go my own way. And that's when I got the motivation to succeed, just go my own way.

Q: Was that a difficult choice?
A: Yes, it was hard; it was really hard, because I still wanted to hang out, but I found that within myself I wasn't happy, and I didn't want to end up in a small town, with four kids, living in a HUD [Department of Housing and Urban Development] home. I didn't want to end up like that. I knew I wanted more for myself. I thought about a future. I was doing really well. I was about to graduate high school, I had a good grade point average, and I made up my mind to get away. It was hard, but I did it. I really did it.

Q: What are they [your peers] doing now?
A: Most of them have two and three kids, and they live with their parents. They never graduated from high school, and, in some cases, the baby's father

is in jail—that basically sums up their lives. They don't have a life, because they have two and three children. They still go to the same risky drinking places, and their behavior is the same.

Q: Are you on your way to fulfilling your aspirations?
A: Yes. I wanted to go to college, and I am now in college. I know that I want to get my master's degree and that will be my next accomplishment. I want to give back to the community and teach. When I was a little girl, I always wanted to teach, and now I know that I can. I know I can do it. It's not that hard; I can do it. If there is a way provided for me, I will do it.

Q: Did Florida Memorial College help you?
A: Yes. I went to a community college before I came to Florida Memorial. Florida Memorial College helped me to become independent. I have family here, but I try to be independent. I'm taking care of myself, and if I make good grades, it's because I want to, and not because I feel like my mother is making me study. I am doing it for myself; it makes me feel independent; I'm taking care of myself.

Q: Does your grandmother still live in this area?
A: No. My grandmother is in Orlando; she moved; my family had moved up there, because my mother got remarried and moved there, so a lot of our family moved, too.

Q: What were the major influences in your life?
A: The number one influence would be God. God helped bring me out of a lot of problem situations, and, then, my grandmother has always been there, and, then, my brother. My brother and I are really close. My father wasn't with us, so my brother was like a father figure in my life. Those are the good people in my life.

Q: Is your father involved with you and your brother now?
A: Yes. I can say he started trying to get involved when I was in high school. But he really didn't do much at all, not really. No.

Q: What activities do you see as being important when growing up?
A: Going to church. Even when I didn't want to go, and my parents made me go. I'm so glad they did, because church was very important. Growing up with a religious foundation, I felt that it was always there for me when I needed it.

Q: Do you pray?
A: Yes. Everyday, everyday, three and four times a day. I always pray. I have been slipping lately, and I have been trying to come back, very important. I try to pray about every little thing. It's very important in my life.

Q: What kinds of things do you ask for in your prayers?
A: First, I thank God; there are a lot of good things going for me, so I thank him for that, and I just ask him to help me keep a straight mind.

Q: Were any other organizations, other than the church, important to you?
A: The choir is important; I used to like to sing. But I am not interested in any other organizations at all.

Q: Are you a member of any organization?
A: No, no, not really. I pretty much like to stay to myself. I have a lot of friends, but I like to stay to myself, because I think it's the best.

Q: What recommendations would you have for young black women in the community?
A: Education. Education is vitally important. One of my friends told me recently that because she had two children at a young age she never thought she would be able to finish her education. But it's possible, anything is possible, if you put God in your life and plan for it.

Q: How old was she when she got pregnant?
A: I think fifteen or sixteen years old.

Q: Did she say why she became pregnant at a young age?
A: She needed somebody to love. She wanted somebody to love. She got pregnant. We had been friends for a while, and I helped her. I was there with her through everything. Then, she got pregnant again. I was really upset with her, but I decided to be by her side again. The baby's father was not anywhere in the picture.

Q: Did the same man father her two children?
A: Yes. She had two boys.

Q: Why do you think young women allow themselves to get pregnant?
A: Most young girls just want unconditional love. Maybe they are not getting feelings of love at home. Another reason is because they feel that's the way to keep a man. They think, "This guy is going to stay with me, we're going to be a family."

Q: Why do the men leave?
A: I couldn't even tell you why they leave. It's just—most of the time—they get tired of the family life, because their girlfriend's pregnancy happens early in the man's life, too—and you know men. Men still want to hang out and have other women on the side. Most of the time, they're just not ready for family life, and they end up leaving.

Q: When you say "unconditional love," do you mean the child loving the mother?
A: Yes. They just want the unconditional love of the child–the same kind of unconditional love that they give the child. Like that.

Q: Do you think that's reality?
A: I really don't feel you have to have a child to have unconditional love, because God is unconditional love, and your parents—most of the time—

everybody's parents. I'm sure that there is one person in the family that you can count on, one person who will give you that unconditional love. You don't have to have a baby at a young age to get unconditional love, because it makes life hard; life becomes too hard.

Q: Was your friend living at home when she became pregnant?
A: Yes. She still lives at home with her parents.

Q: But she's in college?
A: Yes. She's going to a community college; she graduated, got her GED [general equivalency diploma], and [she's] working, working two jobs and taking care her boys.

Q: What thoughts pass through your mind when making a decision?
A: I think of all the negative stuff that people said to me, and all the negative aspects of my life, of my friends' lives, their getting pregnant at an early age, making mistakes, those kinds of thoughts just motivate me to do better, to rise up better than the past. There's nothing that can stop me.

Q: How do you define success?
A: Success is the biggest, the biggest, a really high goal like graduating from college. When I reach that goal it will be everything to me. Reaching a goal is success.

Q: Are there any other thoughts that you would like to share?
A: I just want to share an important factor that I have learned. You can survive in this world without having someone holding you up. That is the main factor.

Q: One more question on young people getting pregnant: are they aware of the fact that they have to protect themselves from getting pregnant?
A: Yes. They're more aware of it now, but they still feel like they want unconditional love, and they want to keep a man. They still believe in the same factors; they still feel that way. They still feel that they have to get pregnant "because that is the only way that I'm going to keep him." You have to love yourself first. Most women don't even love themselves first. That's the biggest problem.

Q: Does it all add up to feelings of being alone, needing love?
A: Yes.

Observer's Comments about Respondent

- self-directed;
- avoids peer pressure;
- interested in helping young children;
- despondent over brother's arrest for murder.

INTERVIEW 2

Q: What factors do you identify as contributing to your success?
A: I identify my mother's persistence in keeping the family together, after having lived through my father's abandonment of the family. I can identify my religion, Christianity, as another strong factor. Also, the friendship of a young man who is my husband.

Q: How did your husband help you through the years?
A: We were friends for ten years before we got married, and he has counseled me, he has comforted me, and he has stood by me.

Q: How old were you when you met your husband?
A: I was fourteen years old. I was in a state of depression, because my father left us; those were my adolescent years. I faced poverty for the first time, and I was discouraged.

Q: Where did you meet your husband?
A: I met my husband on a school bus. As we got to know each other, I saw in him someone who wouldn't abandon or betray me. I learned from him; I learned that I should depend on myself more than on another person.

Q: Did you have troubled experiences with men?
A: Yes. Before I met my husband, I had my first teenage crush. I was just beginning high school, but it was not a happy relationship for me. He judged me by my social class. That was the first time that I was ever exposed to a person who looked at class status, lower and higher class, rich and poor. I did not fit the category that he was looking for; I didn't have expensive clothes or wear jewelry. That was the first time that I faced the reality of being "poor."

Q: Can you identify any obstacles to achieving?
A: Fear and obligations to my family. Fear about moving on and trying new things, taking chances and stepping out, and having confidence and faith in myself. Fear has been an obstacle for me. The absence of a father and a sense of responsibility in the home is an obstacle. I was working to try to help my mother make ends meet, and I was afraid to start school early, or to leave home—to leave the nest—because I felt that I had to help finish the unfinished business that my father left behind.

Q: You felt that responsibility?
A: Yes. I helped raise the children while my mother worked at night, and I grew up pretty fast, faster than my sisters and my brothers.

Q: How did your sisters cope with family matters?
A: They chose paths that were detrimental to their lives. My two older sisters became single parents. They were supposed to be my role models, but they definitely hindered me, because I felt I was the only one to keep the family

going. I wasn't free to pursue my own dreams, my own aspirations; I felt I let go of some of my own potential. My own potential has been dormant, because of my strong sense of obligation to my family.

Q: What are your sisters doing now?
A: Those sisters who were supposed to set an example for me birthed numerous children to different fathers that they did not marry. Presently, they look back and see their mistakes, and they're working now and providing for their children. They're in stable relationships, and they admit and recognize what they've done. They encourage me not to follow in their paths. So I guess I can say that they have learned a little about life and have improved.

Q: Did any of your sisters get married?
A: No. They are not married.

Q: How old are they?
A: Thirty-one and twenty-five years.

Q: What kinds of positions do they hold?
A: The oldest one is a "job jumper," but somehow she takes care of her responsibilities. She goes from one job to another; the other sister is a manager of a local fast-food franchise, and she currently has custody of all of her children and is engaged to be married.

Q: How many children does she have?
A: The one who works at a fast-food place has four children. The oldest sister has three, and both of them are now church oriented. The church is like a garden where they are experiencing growth and understanding and self-exploration. That's my view of their situations presently, based on what they've said and the changes that I've seen in their lives.

Q: Are you friendly with them?
A: Yes.

Q: Do they live in Miami?
A: No. They live in our original home, Dayton, Ohio.

Q: What courses of action have you taken to overcome the obstacles that you perceive? What works for you?
A: I invest a lot of thought in my intentions. I ask other people who have traveled a similar road for their advice.

Q: Why do you think your sisters got pregnant young [and] without being married?
A: I think that they were searching for the love that they should have had from their father, and they probably view marriage as a institution that didn't work anyway. Maybe their ideas of marriage [were] based on the marriages that they saw—for instance, their own parents' marriage—why then should they

gothrough the same ordeal? Women look at themselves in relation to their mothers; we were left alone like a bunch of bastards; we were abandoned. Maybe they lost faith or confidence in the idea of a man being supportive and staying around.

Q: Why do you think your father abandoned his family?
A: I think that it was easier for him to abandon his family than to face some unresolved issues from his childhood. He was abandoned by his mother, and he grew up to disregard women as equals or as partners. He was very chauvinistic, and he took advantage of the strength he had over a woman.

Q: Did his mother ever play a role in bringing him up?
A: Probably the first five to six years of his life, but he lived with his father, and he was raised by his stepmother. His stepmother was submissive to her husband. My father's view of women was not a positive one.

Q: Do you communicate with him now?
A: I've learned through communicating with him that he is human and capable of mistakes just as I am, and I hope that if I ever cause a problem to my children that they will forgive me, as I have forgiven my father.

Q: How old were you when he left?
A: He left when I was thirteen years old.

Q: What (or who) has been the major influence (or influences) in your life?
A: Family, church, and the relationship that I have with my husband.

Q: How long have you been married?
A: Five months.

Q: Did your peers have an influence on you?
A: I was aloof with people. I've never been too sociable; I probably had two friends outside of my relationship with my husband, who was then my boyfriend. I had two friends, but I felt that I was more of a friend to them than they were to me.

Q: Were you involved in athletics?
A: No. My depression as a result of my father's leaving the family caused me to go into a state of withdrawal, and I began to stay home, and eat, and I never developed any athletic skill.

Q: What did food satisfy?
A: It satisfied my hunger, and it took my mind off the things that were bothering me. I thought that I should eat as much as I could when the food was available, because there was never enough food. When we had food, it went like running water.

Q: Does the church play a role in your life?
A: The church calms me. When I go to church, I feel like I have a family, and I associate myself with people who have had problem lives, so I can learn

from them. It also gives me the opportunity to sympathize with others and to know that I am not the only one in the world who suffers. It seems that people suffer—it is human to suffer. Church makes me accept life and appreciate the "ups" and live through the "downs." Church is like the rain, and I am the grass. Church helps me grow.

Q: If you had to choose one role model in your life, who would that be?
A: I would say it is my mother. She's the reason we survived; she worked full time. Even when she didn't have a job, she kept her head up; she didn't give us up to [foster care]; she didn't abandon or forsake us. She continued to set an example. She proved to me that no matter what comes along, you can still be strong; you don't have to let things change you for the worse; you can survive the obstacles.

Q: What type of work does she have now?
A: She works in an office; she does secretarial work.

Q: What recommendations would you have for younger black women in the community?
A: I recommend that they treat themselves to reading literature written by black women, so that they can understand their history and learn about the strengths of black women. Also, I recommend that they pursue their hopes and dreams.

Q: In the black literature course that you took, what did you learn?
A: I learned about the character of black women–their ability to cope and make a life for their children. Also, the poets' use of imagery and the realness of settings and experiences–the literature reflects the black experience in this country, and all black women can relate to the stories and understand themselves better.

Q: Do you relate your present-day dilemmas [to] what happened to black women of the past in slavery? Is that part of your consciousness?
A: Yes. It's a part of my consciousness. The feelings of being an outsider, not part of America, still remains. I never noticed my color until I was in a neighborhood surrounded by white people and they [said] horrible things to me. I had a bad experience coming home from school. A white boy pushed me down while I was crossing the street, and he called me "nigger," and he and other boys tried to keep me in the street while a truck was coming. They tried to get me run over, but I got up in time to escape death.

Q: How do you resolve something like that in your mind?
A: Well, I repressed it, and I lived through it, so I count my blessings.

Q: What additional advice can you share with young black women?
A: I recommend that young black women [be] very selective and observant when choosing mates so that their children, especially girls, will grow up

feeling secure and confident about themselves. It's important to have a caring mother, but without a father, a girl doesn't really know where to begin, what to accept from a man, how to relate, what to tolerate. She needs a father who will love her and protect her and teach her never to accept abuse or violence. Too many women are victims of domestic violence. This could be the consequences of seeing their fathers beat their mothers, or being in a home where there was no father to lead them in a positive direction. Single parenting is not working. We need to come together to see how we can improve relationships amongst our young. We need proper guidance at home—mothers and fathers that set good examples.

Q: Did you have a sense of not being protected when your father left?
A: Yes, I did. The lack of a man leaves a woman vulnerable.

Q: What thoughts pass through your mind when you make a decision?
A: Whether it's a good decision for me, how it will affect me, how it will affect the people around me, and the benefit or result in the long run.

Q: What is inside you that motivates you to succeed?
A: Hope and the thirst for knowledge. Success is not the acquiring of tangible goods, but it is knowledge. It is also a spiritual understanding, and self-discovery, and knowledge that I can share with people that I care about. Some matters transcend the physical. Pride, love, self-acceptance [are] motivating. I am motivated by abstract qualities.

Q: Do you wish to add any other insights to this interview?
A: Yes. I want to add that black women do feel positive about themselves. Now, I believe, that black men need to really feel positive about themselves. It is an individual pursuit. Achievement gives positive feelings. Obtaining an education, credentials that open doors, helping children in the neighborhood, serving country—if good things happen to black men, black women and families will also benefit. We need to give hope to black men.

Observer's Comments about Respondent

- lingering depression as a result of father leaving the family;
- identifies with mother, who is a survivor despite hardships;
- devoted to her grandmother, who is presently ill;
- church gives her solace.

INTERVIEW 3

Q: What factors do you identify as contributing to your success?
A: One of the main factors that contributed to my college success is my faith in God and his faith in me. I believe in God, and I believe that he cares about

me. I believe in prayer, and I believe in myself. When I set out to accomplish something, I never give up. I can go to college; I can do well in college, I can get my degree. I know all of that. I just have to draw on my strength, the strength that God gave to me. My grandmother would be the second strength that I can draw from. She has always been very supportive. She strongly advocates an education. She was born in 1920, and, at that time, there were not many opportunities to get an education. So, here I am, and she says "Go for it." I feel fortunate to have my grandmother in my corner to cheer for me.

Q: What were your greatest obstacles to your success?
A: A bad mind-set, wrong thinking. It wasn't teachers or professors or my peers. It had to have been a negative outlook on the potential that was inside of me; it wasn't something external. Most of my obstacles were my own feelings about myself; I had to overcome my own feelings

Q: What didn't you like about yourself?
A: I thought that I wasn't worthy of getting a college degree, or I wasn't good enough to have good things in my life. My mom didn't get a college education, nor did my dad, so I didn't have good examples, and I felt "low" about myself.

Q: Do you feel young people need role models or motivators?
A: I really believe that children need patterns, examples to draw strength from, to draw ideals from, to draw goals from. In my case, I had a grandmother, who wasn't educated, but there was a lot of love and warmth in the house. Even though she advised me to get an education, she didn't know the steps to take to get an education. From my own experience, I definitely agree that children need examples in their lives—educational, spiritual—they need those examples.

Q: What courses of action have you taken to overcome the obstacles that you encountered, for example, your own feelings of low self-esteem?
A: I prayed. I turned to God as my spiritual guide, but I was also practical in my daily life. I set goals and worked on strategies to obtain the goals, first small goals, then bigger goals. It has been a growing process, a maturing process. Through the small achievement to the bigger achievements, I soon was on my way. It worked. When I achieved my goal, I felt stronger, and I felt proud inside. I also felt that my grandmother was proud of me—that was important to me. I had to break the cycle of negative thinking in order to grow.

Q: Could you give an example of one of the negative patterns that you decided to break?
A: One of the patterns that I needed to change was my own interpersonal relationships, specifically with men. I felt that I needed a boyfriend and that my worth was determined by having a boyfriend. Again, I started to pray, and I directed my thoughts to God. I said, "I want to feel good about myself; I am too dependent on having a boyfriend; I need to learn how to get along without

a boyfriend." By stating my problem, I realized that I could help myself, and I started on a routine to do nice things by myself or with girlfriends, and it did work eventually. I set up routines to make myself acknowledge myself. I bought myself flowers; I would go out to the movies with a group of my girlfriends; I would recognize the positive things about myself. I slowly changed, because I didn't dwell on the negative all the time.

Q: One of your very positive attributes is your ability to communicate; you have a great gift for expressing what you mean. Did you have to develop that ability, or did it come naturally?

A: It came naturally. I became aware of my oratorical skills when I was ten years old. I had to recite a little poem as part of an Easter program at church. Since that time, I have had no problem getting up to speak; I've never been afraid. It amazes me sometimes when I am at different events, people will ask me to speak; I never know what I am going to say, but when I get to the podium, the words just flow out of me; I really believe it is a gift of God.

Q: Do you feel reticent about speaking?
A: Not at all. Not at all.

Q: Did you get any training through church participation?
A: No. They said, "Hey this girl can talk!" She knows how to enunciate and pronounce words, and at eleven years old, various church folk entered me into oratorical contests. Speeches had to be five to seven minutes long; someone would write the speech, and, then, they would give it to me and tell me to memorize it. I would memorize it. When I practiced the speech, they would tell me where to slow down and where to stop, but other than that, I had no training. That was about it.

Q: Has that fluency helped you in college?
A: I'm not sure. Well, maybe, I am Ms. Florida Memorial College, and I have to represent the college in speaking engagements, and I am not afraid to speak in public. I also think it helps a lot when I have to do presentations in class; everyone sits and looks at me like, "Whoa, man, where did that come from?" But it is something that comes so naturally to me. I can't even describe it. I'm sure it will pay off in the long run, because I do plan on talking for a living. I plan on traveling and talking; I'm not sure of the big picture yet, but I am sure that I will figure it out.

Q: What are your goals?
A: My goal is to get a doctorate degree in counseling. That's my goal now. It's not etched in stone, because I don't know what opportunities will pop up in front of me, but my goal is to be an international traveler and renowned world speaker.

Q: What topic would you speak about?
A: Self-help. I would always tell my story. I would tell other young women that even if you are from a single-parent home with low income [or] problematic circumstances, similar to mine, don't give up on yourself. Your life will

not be perpetually negative, if you do not give up on yourself. I would set out a path for them, show them the way.

Q: Do you feel that you are a cheerleader?
A: Absolutely. Absolutely. I never have to be out front. I never have to be in the forefront to present the big picture. I love sitting in the corner and rooting on other people who think they can't do it, and I'm just a little cheerleader in the corner saying, "Go man, you can do it." Sometimes that's all a person needs, someone to believe that they can do it. It may take two seconds of my time, but it can last a lifetime in a person's memory. They'll step out and do things that no one ever imagined.

Q: Besides your grandmother, who were the major influences in your life?
A: Well, it may sound funny to say this, but my mom was an influence, because I always knew that she was the type of woman that I wouldn't want to be. My mom is my mom, and we are quite a bit alike. My mom can talk to anybody. She's intelligent; she can fit into any social group, but she really never applied herself, and I think her gifts and talents went unused. But I had a positive example in my grandmother, even without an education, she was a positive example to me.

Q: Is she working presently?
A: My mom? Yes, she is working for the Red Cross. She helps homeless people. My mom is a very sweet lady. We had some very difficult times when I was growing up. She abused drugs, and, actually, she was a call girl; she was a prostitute living in the same house as my sister and me. Because of the years of drug abuse, I really believe she has developed a chemical imbalance, but she's a sweet lady and I love her, and I've learned a lot from her. I really did.

Q: What did you learn?
A: I learned that a man is not the center of a woman's life. I learned that God should be the center; put him first and do things through his strength, and if you meet a man who does not encourage you to get an education, or encourage you to pursue your dreams, then do not have him as part of your life. Basically, that was part of the reason for my having a low self-esteem, because of the pattern that I saw in front of me. I thought that I needed a man like my mom did; that was a pattern that had to be broken over time, so I won't say it's perfected 100 percent, but I think it's perfected 99.9 percent, and I think I'm doing OK.

Q: What is your mother doing now? Does your mother have someone now?
A: She has a job, and she bought herself a car, so she's doing well; she's doing better now than she did twenty years ago, and I am proud of that. She just graduated from an educational program where she can work at a day care center, if she [wants] to, so I'm proud of the progress that my mom has made. No, she's not with a man right now.

Q: Did any teachers influence you?

A: The one teacher that influenced me the most, I hated the most. His name was [Mr. L. G.]; he was my band director. He was always pushing me to the next level, and his method of doing things was quite unorthodox compared to what we're being told by professionals today, but he was always pushing me to the next level. Then, I had a teacher here at college, who I hated, well, *hate* is such a strong word, maybe I shouldn't use it, but I didn't like going to his class, because he would always pick on me. I would raise my hand to ask a question, and he would say, "No. Ms. D. that's enough from you, we've heard enough." But, his way of pushing made me come back to class even more sharp on the material. So Mr. G. and Mr. E. were very influential.

Q: What should a teacher do to motivate a student?

A: All students aren't the same, and the best thing any teacher could do for any student would be to assume that they know absolutely nothing. Many teachers teach as if they are teaching colleagues; students are not on that level. Some students may come from homes that have printed material available, and they see their parents reading. Other students may come from homes where the parents are always working, and the children, basically, raise themselves. Teachers will be the most effective if they review basic material, then slowly proceed to the level [at which students] should be taught; they, then, can tell which students need extra help. Also, teachers should know their students and be able to judge the students on more than an exam and help the student who needs extra attention; teachers need to put their hearts into teaching.

Q: What is your major?

A: Elementary education.

Q: Were you involved in athletics while growing up?

A: Yes. I played basketball, and I was in the marching band. I always liked being athletic. I also ran track for one quarter when I was in junior high school.

Q: Do you still participate in athletics?

A: No. I'm not athletic now at all, but I do quite a bit of walking. I'm not sure if that counts, but I do quite a bit of walking.

Q: Every day?

A: Not every day, except I do walk from my dorm to my classes and all around the campus, but to actually time myself and say, "I'm going to do a forty-five-minute walk to get my heart rate up—no, I don't do that right now."

Q: Where were you born?

A: I was born in Fort Lauderdale.

Q: Could you describe the home that you grew up in?

A: The home that I grew up in was a place that felt so warm, yet strict. I stayed with my grandmother and my grandfather. They were very supportive in the organizational activities that I wanted to get involved in. There were strict rules, and I had to obey the rules. They would say, "I don't have to explain to you why I want you to do this or that, just know that the rules are good for you." I had both warmth and discipline when I was growing up. Nevertheless, I now know why the rules had to be set.

Q: What thoughts pass through your mind when you have to make a decision?
A: I think about my unborn children. I think about how the decision will affect my children. For instance, "Will investing in this mutual fund help them later on; will getting a master's or doctor's degree add to their legacy? Will going to the basketball game instead of doing my homework affect them?" I always think about my kids, my unborn kids, that aren't even here yet. I always think about them.

Q: Do those thoughts about raising children go back to your relationship with your mother and how she affected you?
A: Yes. Absolutely. It took a long, long time for me to understand what happened to my mother. Those years when she decided that my grandmother should have legal guardianship of her children. How heartbreaking that must have been for her, as a mom, to admit that she was not mentally, financially, and/or socially capable enough to raise two girls. Two little girls. I am sure that the decisions that I make now are in direct reflection of the heartbreak and the pain that I saw my mom go through and that I felt as a little girl, and, of course, I don't want to bring those kinds of incidents and feelings in on my own children. At the same time, I've heard people say, "I'm not going to be like my mom," or "I'm not going to be like my dad," yet end up being just like them, because what they experienced as a child was deeply embedded in them.

Q: Do you think an abused child becomes a parent who inflicts abuse?
A: Yes. It happens. But we have to stop placing the blame on the parent. It was something that happened, and, of course, it has serious ramifications for future behavior, but, at some point, individuals have to take control of their own lives, and at some point, have to say: "This is my life now, and I get to decide how I live the next seventy or eighty years. So, therefore I'm going to do everything I know how to make good quality decisions throughout my life." There has to be a turning point, a cut-off point where a person "rights the wrongs" of the past. Improving behavior is practice; you have to practice being good to yourself and others every day.

Q: What is inside you that motivates you to succeed?
A: My unborn kids. My unborn kids, and I want to be somebody. Maybe being someone who makes a difference to someone else; maybe being the best schoolteacher. Being "somebody" is being the best mom and the best wife in the whole wide world. Many young women my age are really driven by getting their degree, money, and nice cars—which is good, there's nothing

wrong with that; I am not saying that I don't want a nice car—but, to me, having a husband that loves me and respects my gifts and talents, and to have children who are happy, is like a prize, a gift, and something that you have to plan for.

Q: What organizations or activities do you identify as being important to your development?
A: Well, I do a lot of reading; being in college now, I read out of necessity. Other activities that are important: I used to sing in the gospel choir. Singing makes me feel good; if you are feeling down, get yourself a nice song going, and you feel good.

Q: What recommendations do you have for younger black women in the community?
A: My recommendation would be to hook up with someone that you admire, who is a professional—that person could be a cook in a restaurant, teacher, or politician. But hook up with someone who can guide you into to making good quality decisions concerning education and your social life. In the inner city, where low income families live, there are many types of negative examples, and the girls tend to follow the pattern that they see in front of them. I don't mean that what they see is bad, but it could be bad; there is so much out there, such a wealth of information that young black women could miss out on—the good information. So, my recommendation would be to hook up with someone who can give positive mentoring and give good, sound educational advice.

Q: Are you acquainted with girls that get pregnant young and become a single parent?
A: Yes. Quite a few of them. Some of them had their baby and ended up having to raise the baby by themselves and didn't graduate high school. Some did graduate high school, and there were a couple of them, unmarried with a baby, who were just tough soldiers who did go to college, and graduated, and became professionals. One young girl that I know became a pharmacist. I think it's the fight within, the determination. It all boils down to making decisions. Are you willing to count up the cost of being somebody? It's easy to sit around and get a check from the government. That's not too hard; it really doesn't take much at all. But the determination to go to school may take a lot, dragging the kids along—but isn't it worth the cost for the benefits in the future? It involves hard decisions. Having babies and striking out on your own takes courage. Some girls are afraid, or they think it's too hard.

Q: Why do you think these young women have children out of wedlock?
A: I don't know. Maybe they think it's cute to be twenty years old with five and six kids. These girls need to be educated on the facts of life. Let me give you a scenario: if you have a ten-year-old girl, and she has a mentor that begins to take her to different places, and begins to calibrate her mind to

different opportunities outside of the inner city, then she will have a picture to draw from— some type of image—and, hopefully, begin to think about building another life. Many young women get caught up in a trap that they never escape from. They get involved in a relationship with a young man, have children, and just blow it. These young women need to feel that they have choices: the choice of whether to have children or not, the choice of whether to get an education or not—instead of just being blinded by the 'hood's [neighborhood's] world.

Q: Did you have a vision of getting out of the inner city?
A: No. I just decided that I wanted to go to college. I know it may sound crazy, but my decision to go to college was based on the fact that I wanted to make money. I didn't want to be poor. I didn't want to live in the projects. I wanted to have a home and drive a nice car. But now I'm a big girl, and I understand that education is more than getting a paycheck.

Q: Can you expand on what you mean?
A: It's a continual exploration. It's a continual wealth of knowledge; even after you get your degree, there's still so much that you don't know. Education is a process. You live the experience and graduate. You get your credentials, then, the next week, you turn on the television and learn that something brand new happened in the field that you graduated from. It's like an ongoing evolution of knowledge. It's pretty neat.

Observer's Comments about Respondent

- experienced her mother's degradation through drug abuse and prostitution;
- realized early on that obtaining an education would uplift her;
- thinks about her "unborn" children, and the effect on them, when she makes a decision;
- plans for the future include a husband who has the same goals.

INTERVIEW 4

Q: What factors do you identify as contributing to your success?
A: Myself first, along with my mother, my grandmother, and my teachers, both past and present.

Q: Can you give me examples of how your mother motivated you?
A: She motivated me by speaking to me; she was very open. We had a very good relationship. The communication was at a high level throughout all my growing years, and, even now, I always go to her for advice.

Q: Could you give me an example of what you discuss?
A: Life in general. She taught me how to get along with different people, maintain a good attitude, and communicate effectively. My father was not an

easy person to talk with, and he would always upset me. I would try to talk to him, and he wasn't very open with me. She continued to coach me through my confrontations with him, and, instead of destroying me, I was able to turn situations around to benefit me.

Q: How did your grandmother help?
A: Well, my grandmother was the in-between person. She never took sides. She gave her opinion, and she was another listening ear. Her role was trying to make sure that my mother—I was being raised by my mom—wouldn't teach me to hate my father, that she wouldn't teach me to dislike people because of the relationship that I had with my father. Grandma was the one that didn't take sides. She allowed me to make my own choices, my own decisions. She reminded me that in handling any issue . . . I needed to look at both sides before I acted.

Q: Did your father help in raising you?
A: No.

Q: When did he leave the house?
A: He left the house when I was two years of age, and my parents were divorced when I turned eight years old. They were separated for six years.

Q: Did they live in the same community?
A: Yes. But I never saw my father.

Q: He never came to see you?
A: No.

Q: Do you communicate with him now?
A: As I got older, I made several attempts to see him, and there were times that I did see him. When I graduated from high school, I didn't want to invite him, because it was my victory, my special day, and I felt as if he didn't have anything to do with me up until that point, so I didn't want him there. My grandmother, on the other hand, said that I should invite him—that it was up to him to make the decision to attend or not. I eventually invited him, and he did come. Although it was my day, I think that his presence took away from it, because I didn't want him there. Recently, I haven't heard from him. Well, I spoke to him about a month ago and that was only because I called him. He has never initiated any communication with me. He never tries to make any contact with me.

Q: Do you know why?
A: No. Actually, I don't. I know that he is married and that he has two younger children, but I have absolutely no knowledge of why he wouldn't want to make me a part of my life. He doesn't want me; he doesn't want to be there for me and to help me along the way, but when I've achieved a goal, or when I reach a certain point of celebration, then he wants to be included.

Q: In retrospect, how do you feel about your father?
A: I love him, because he's my father, and I respect him, because he's my father, but as a person, I don't particularly care for him. He has shown me, on many occasions, that he does not accept responsibility; I feel that he left a project undone in me. However, if I ever decide to have children, I will thank him for the detrimental experiences that he exposed me to—those negative experiences that I will look to avoid when I bring up my own children.

Q: When you think about your father, what is your candid reaction?
A: I get upset. I get a negative reaction. As a parent, I would act differently than what he subjected me to as a child growing up, as a girl growing up.

Q: What do you think you missed not having a father in the home?
A: Well, when I look at my peers now—my best friend has a two-parent home—when I let it touch me emotionally, I am jealous. I have never experienced the happiness that I see in her. I could say that I never felt complete; I could say that I hurt. I feel like I was the one that really suffered in the entire situation, and I don't understand what I did, or what the problems were—how bad a circumstance—wherein my father would not want to be in the same home with his family.

Q: Did he visit?
A: No. He could have at least visited. But, there were different means of communicating, too, which he never used. When I look at the entire situation, I can say one positive factor that came out of his behavior toward me and that is I grew closer to my mother. I have a strong bond with her. Even now, I celebrate Father's Day with my mom, and I take my mom out, so she gets two holidays a year. She gets Mother's Day and Father's Day, and I have great respect for her, because she did it on her own. She raised me without my father's help.

Q: How did she accomplish bringing up her children without support?
A: It was very hard, and I can say that, even now, it is still very hard; I can see her struggle everyday, but I understand her situation much more now. My grandmother helped her when we moved here. My grandmother helped her by getting involved with the care of the children. My mother always worked; she always worked long days, ten and twelve hours a day. When we discuss the past—the problems that she had—she says that when she looked at her family, and knowing what she wanted for them, gave her the strength and drive to continue.

Q: What type of work does your mother do?
A: Currently, she is employed by the Dade County Public Schools as an administrative secretary.

Q: Did she pursue an education after high school?
A: She did. She got her Associate of Arts degree, but I think that she reached her position strictly by experience.

Q: Did your grandmother work?
A: My grandmother was a foster mom in her younger days, and she did light housework. Also, she was a midwife. Actually, she never had to work. My grandfather was the provider, and after he passed, she received funds from the state, Social Security.

Q: Did your grandparents live in the home with you?
A: No.

Q: Did they take care of you some of the time?
A: Yes. Sometimes, I would spend weekends with my grandparents, and my grandmother would usually pick me up after school; I would stay at her house until my mom got off from work.

Q: What factors do you identify as obstacles to your success?
A: When I spoke about the contributing factors, I named myself as one. I look at my peers, and those around me, particularly African Americans, that blame other people, other races for holding them down, but, in reality, those feelings need to be overcome within the person. Each person needs to determine his or her own success rate, own success factors. The biggest obstacle for me was not to allow myself to have that chain of thought—to continue everyday. I continue to work hard and to put my best foot forward in society, as I step along. I make my own path. We need to learn how to look at the big picture. Being nonproductive is no one else's fault. You need to put the blame on yourself.

Q: What thoughts pass through you mind when you have to make a decision?
A: Well, I think about how it's going to benefit me now, if it will hurt me in the long run, and, most of all, I think about who else the decision will affect. I know no matter what decision I make I have to wake up with it; I have to be able to look at myself and respect myself afterwards.

Q: When you were a teenager, did any of your friends get pregnant without getting married?
A: Yes.

Q: Would you tell us about their lives?
A: Yes. Actually, the majority of my high school girlfriends, seven out of ten, are either pregnant now or have had a child, and I can't remember any of them that have married.

Q: What is the average age that they got pregnant?
A: I would say between seventeen and twenty, mostly seventeen and eighteen.

Q: Why do you think they allowed that to happen, didn't protect themselves?
A: I can say that they wanted to get pregnant, because they didn't feel loved at home, and they wanted unchallenged love. Another reason may be that, as young ladies, we look for love in the wrong places. I have a friend that has

been trying to get pregnant; she wants to direct her love somewhere. She feels that she has been wronged by people; she's been caught up in difficult relationships; now she is twenty years old and pregnant. I can't understand why she would want to be pregnant, or why she would want to bring a child into the world. But that's what she wanted to do for quite some time, and now she will have her baby.

Q: Is her boyfriend taking any responsibility for the child?
A: No. As a matter of fact, the guy that got her pregnant is no longer her boyfriend. She is staying at home with her mom. Her parents have just separated, and I know this will add more stress to the family. She is just home. She is not taking care of herself; she doesn't work; she is just home. Her mom and her family have to take part in taking care of this child.

Q: Why would a young woman want to complicate her life?
A: I have no idea.

Q: Was she ever productive?
A: She had been productive at one point; she was staying on her own, and she was working a full time job. She dropped out of high school. She had hoped to go back to school, and earn a GED, and maybe continue an education through correspondence courses, or pick up a trade. However, I don't see where she has achieved any of that. I don't understand why she wanted to get pregnant, or why she would want to bring a child into this world. She has not done anything that would provide security for herself or the child. I don't see what she has to offer a newborn baby, or a growing child.

Q: Is it possible she wanted to drop out of society?
A: Anything is possible. I can't say for sure. I don't know.

Q: Do you think she wanted unconditional love from a little child? Would that have made her feel complete?
A: I think that it would have given her some form of satisfaction, but, in thinking that way, she would have to be totally selfish, because she would be thinking of herself, and not the child.

Q: You mentioned teachers and family that influenced your life. What about peers? Did they influence your life in any way?
A: My peers would have influenced me by the daily contact that I had with them in school. We were on the same school level, but we definitely didn't think alike. The real influence was my reaction to the way they lived their lives, because I began to learn what I didn't want to be, and that made me go in the opposite direction. That is the best way for me to describe the way in which they influenced me.

Q: Were you involved in the church?
A: Yes.

Q: Did that help you through your young years?
A: I can say that it did. I don't think that it's the church itself that helps. Because I've learned in the church that it's hard to understand how people profess a religion, and a belief in Christ, yet there's so much bigotry within the church. So, I don't feel comfortable saying that the church has helped me, but I can say that my belief in God and my personal values have helped me.

Q: Were you influenced by attending church services?
A: No. My influences were in reading and understanding the Bible—the way in which our lives should be lived.

Q: Did the Bible give you rules for good conduct in life?
A: Yes.

Q: What organizations do you identify as being important to your development?
A: I'm not really involved in any specific organizations. On a monthly basis, I volunteer my time in homeless shelters. I also make donations to the Salvation Army and Camillus House [homeless shelter] when I can.

Q: When you volunteer in the homeless shelters, how do you help?
A: We feed the homeless. I have taken groceries, clothes; I have talked to the young girls about taking care of their health and personal hygiene. At this time, I feel that I am good at sharing my ideas and opinions, so I do. I know that I also make these women feel good about themselves, and they need to have their self-esteem bolstered; speaking to them also makes me feel good about myself.

Q: If I walked into a shelter what would I see?
A: When I walked in, I saw individuals that have lost hope, and they need a booster shot of hope, of encouragement; they need someone to help push them forward. Very rarely do you run into someone in the shelter that wants everything done for them. I think that all they need is just a push. I encourage them, and I talk to them about job training and finding a suitable position. I tell them that they must wear the right attire and be prepared for the job. In many different cases, preparations have been made for them, and they go on, and they do for themselves.

Q: Do they become contributing members of society?
A: Yes. They get assistance in finding work and becoming a part of society. There is also housing assistance. But I run into many people, generally the older set—50 and above—who have completely lost hope, and it is really hard, because some of them can't read, some of them can't write. They don't know anything else but to be there, and I don't consider them hopeless. I just think that they need to be helped more than others. I think that if given the right encouragement, they, too, can become a meaningful part of society. Someone needs to be there and walk them through.

Q: Do you think many them have drug and/or alcohol problems?
A: Yes. Being on the street, there is not much to turn to, and because they are vulnerable, they are willing to subject themselves to what comes along, good or bad.

Q: If the women need money, will they become prostitutes?
A: Yes. even prostitution, anything for money. Anything for money, because money is something that they want. I run into cases where people have tried to sell their children. They will sell their souls. When these women try to get on the right track, and try to find their children, they can't find them. Their children are gone, their bodies are wrecked; once the losses come to that point, they really don't know what to do, or where to go.

Q: What do they use the money for?
A: What I've heard is that they use the money for drugs and alcohol. They use the money for food, too, but they can't save it [money]. Being out on the street, there is no protection. They can easily be robbed, so they spend the money as they go, sometimes for food, mostly for drugs and alcohol.

Q: What was the emotional climate in your home when you were growing up?
A: I have two younger brothers; emotionally, it was tiring, it was stressful, because both my brothers and I wanted more, and we didn't understand values. It was stressful on my mom; she wanted to give us more; she felt that we deserved more. But the strongest factor in my house was love; my house was filled with love; my home was also filled with understanding, if nothing else.

Q: Do your brothers have the same father as you do?
A: No. They have two different fathers.

Q: Did their fathers contribute to the household in any way?
A: No.

Q: Did your mother marry again?
A: She married again, but that didn't work either. I think that my mother went through emotional turmoil; she was emotionally drained. She needed to take the time to sort out her life, decide what she wanted, instead of taking whatever comes along. She continues to subject herself on a wish—on a wish that maybe this time it won't be the same, it will be better.

Q: Have you learned anything from your mother's experiences?
A: Well, I, too, have made mistakes, and I have been in rough relationships. I'm not currently involved with anyone on any level; I want to take time for myself. I want to get my life together, and I don't feel like I need to be involved with anyone in my life right now. I think having someone, at this time, would be detrimental to my achieving. People have to look out for themselves—that is what I am doing now. I am looking out for myself. I don't

have to think about what someone else needs from me, or what I need from someone else. I don't want to complicate my life. I want to concentrate on my education and get ahead. By the time I graduate from college and medical school, I will be mature enough, hopefully, to make careful decisions. It's not a rush; it's not a rush. My involvement in a relationship is something for the future; there is no urgency about it. When I meet someone, it will come together easily; it's nothing that I will try to make happen, and I think that type of thinking will lead me to a good choice.

Q: What is the greatest obstacle an African American woman has to overcome?
A: The African American man. I say that because the African American woman is a strong, strong, very strong, strong-minded independent woman. I think that is how she was born. I think that men realize it, and they try to strip the woman of that strength, and, no matter what you hear or what you go through in life, that is something that a woman needs to keep in mind. Independence is second nature. It's something the woman knows, and I think that when she has that knowledge within, when she knows what it is, and is sure of what it she wants, and what it is that she expects out of life, then no one, no man of any race, nation, or culture can take that from her, and, I think, that is subconsciously the goal of men—to strip a woman of her independence.

Q: Do you think that the conflicted male/female relationship, as you describe [previously,] is uniquely African American, or that problematic relationships cross all cultures?
A: I would say that this dynamic crosses cultures—any male/female relationship—men and women of any race, of any culture.

Q: What recommendations would you have for younger black women in the community?
A: My only recommendation would be to look into yourself. You have to decide early what it is that you want for yourself. If you decide that you want a house, with a white picket fence, family, and dog, and that your goal is to make $200,000 a year, then, that is what you should work for. You have to decide that early–achievement is progressive. You can't wait until you are thirty-five years old to start planning for the future. You can't waste your teenage years. You can't go through young adulthood goofing off, and do whatever you think you are big and bad enough to do. A good life is preparation; it is very progressive, it is a level of succession. You have to sow the seeds young; you have to train yourself to have the discipline to go forward. Do you want to become a queen of some country, or do you want to be a "queen" period? What you need to do is—behave like a princess, and, eventually, you will be that queen you want to be.

Observer's Comments about Respondent

- often speaks about her goal, medical school;

- feels that the African American woman is born with inner strength;
- resents her father for neglecting her when times were tough.

INTERVIEW 5

Q: What factors do you identify as contributing to your success?
A: My upbringing, my family, definitely my mother, [was] a main source of my success. She believes in me so much that I couldn't let her down, and I had to accomplish positive goals for her, even if I felt that I didn't want to—I couldn't let her down. So that's one of the biggest pushes besides social—the social push of having to go to college to be successful contributes to pushing you ahead, too. You have to go to college these days to get any type of decent job, and these days you not only have to get the bachelor's degree, but you also have to get your master's degree—preparing yourself for the future, that is a strong influence.

Q: What is your major?
A: English education

Q: Why did you choose education?
A: I chose education because of my need to help children. In high school, I was not a bad student, but I was troubled. Now, I feel the need to help other troubled students. I started to major in ESE [Exceptional Student Education], then I took an English class and decided that I wanted to change my major.

Q: Could you tell us about your family? Is your father living with the family?
A: Yes, my father has always lived with us; he still lives with us, but I cannot say that he has been a major factor in my upbringing. I have read that it is important for a father to be in the home, and my father was in the home; however, he wasn't instrumental in my upbringing. My mother was the biggest factor in my upbringing.

Q: What role does your father play in the family?
A: My father lives with us, but he doesn't play a role. He was always in and out of the house; the role that he plays now is sitting in front of the television [laughing]. Oh no, he hasn't played a role in the family.

Q: Did any of your grandmothers have a role in your upbringing?
A: The only ties that I have to my family is my mother and my father. I don't know my grandmother on my father's side. She lives in Jamaica; I never met her. My mother's mother passed away when she was eight years old. I have to say that I feel like a person that doesn't have much of a family history. The only history that I have is what I see in front of me—my mother and father.

Q: Could you describe the neighborhood that you grew up in?
A: My neighborhood is predominantly black; the exception is one white family on each block. It's not a bad neighborhood, but you have to be careful.

There was one point in time where a lot of people's houses were being broken into. I remember one time my mother's purse was stolen from the front yard. We have to be careful. But other than that, it's a good neighborhood.

Q: Does your family own the home that you live in?
A: Yes. My family owns the home that we live in; I've lived in the home for twenty-three years. I've never moved; it's my home.

Q: Therefore do you know many people in the neighborhood?
A: I know people that I went to elementary school with, but I don't keep in touch with them, because when I left elementary school, my mother put me in a predominantly white school on the other side of town. For junior high school, I went to a magnet school that was not in my neighborhood. For high school, I went to another magnet school. I did not have the experience of growing up with kids in my neighborhood and going to school with them.

Q: You have a very light complexion. Is your family interracial ?
A: My mother's mother was Indian and Irish. I've seen pictures of my great-grandmother and great-grandfather. My mother is light skinned, but I am lighter than my mother. My father is dark skinned.

Q: Does your light skin color pose a problem for you within the black community?
 A: Yes, yes, yes, yes. My skin complexion is a major factor in relationships that I have with African Americans, in general. They either like me because I'm light skinned, or they don't like me because I'm light skinned. They tend to prejudge me, because of my skin color. I've been called "prissy" and "stuck up." I am a pretty quiet person, and people label me "stuck up." I say, "Well if I wasn't light skinned, and not to be vain, but if I wasn't pretty, then I would just be a shy girl, but because I have those characteristics, I am called 'stuck up.' "

Q: What type of men do you choose to go out with—is color a factor?
A: I'm attracted to dark-skinned men—the darker, the better [laughing]. I'm not attracted to light-skinned men. I don't know why; I don't know why, but I'm just attracted to darker-skinned men.

Q: What factors do you identify as obstacles that you have had to overcome?
A: Violence. I think something that defines me is the death of my two brothers. They both died violently. The result of the breakup of my family has a lot to do with the person I am today. My brothers' violent deaths and my sister being kicked out of my house when I was in the fifth grade left me feeling "alone." Even though I had three siblings, two brothers and one sister, I grew up in the house by myself. So, I consider myself an only child—something that has influenced me a lot.

Q: How did your brothers die?
A: My oldest brother was killed by gunshots to his back. When he was coming home from a date with a girl he took to the movies, guys jumped out of the

bushes of an abandoned house that was next door to my brother's house, and they said, "Nigga we got you ..." or something like that, and they shot him, but they didn't steal any money, so I'm not sure exactly why they killed him. His date told the police the story. My other brother died from a stab wound in the stomach by his girlfriend. It cut his aorta, and he died from internal bleeding. These two killings happened in a three-year span of each other. My mother never got over the murders of my brothers. I try to help her the best that I can. As you can imagine, it is very difficult for us. She is always depressed.

Q: Did the police ever find out who committed the murder of your oldest brother?
A: The street gossip in the neighborhood—the guy that they say did it—got shot about three weeks afterward. It's not the police who said he did it, but everyone else believed he did it.

Q: Did the police ever find out the reason why your youngest brother was stabbed by his girlfriend?
A: I don't know exactly what happened, but she was not charged with his killing. I don't know the facts. It happened in New York. After the funeral, we went back to Miami, and nobody wanted to go back to New York.

Q: Has physical violence been enacted upon you personally?
A: Yes, at one time, my boyfriend became obsessed with me. He wouldn't leave me alone; he pushed me a lot; I couldn't take it anymore. When I graduated from high school, I moved to another state. Also, I remember one time when I came home, I found a man lying on the floor in my kitchen, and I couldn't open the door. I remember that incident like it was yesterday; I was terrified. The ambulance came and took him away. You can say, I experienced both emotional and physical violence.

Q: What courses of action have you taken to overcome the difficulties that you had in your life?
A: I have found strength through spirituality. Sometimes, I don't even know how I pulled through; I just did. I really don't need to know what steps were taken, I cannot even describe how I managed to survive the day—every day. I have to say that I survived through the strength God gave me.

Q: How did your mother live through the violent deaths of her sons?
A: My mother was wrecked. My mom went through some hard times. It is extremely difficult for her, particularly on their birthdays, on the days that they died, and on Mother's Day. Mother's Day is the worst day, the very worst day.

Q: Was your oldest brother shot down by a white man?
A: No. He was shot down by black people. Yeah, he was shot by some brother that he probably said "Hi" to a few days before. That is just how it is.

Q: Why do you think there is so much violence in America today?

A: I know in the black community a lot of brothers are angry, and they're angry because they have a problem with society, police harassment in particular. They do not feel that they are given opportunities like people of other races. They feel that they are outsiders, not really a part of society. They become angry because of that, and some of them just give up. They try to make a way for themselves in the streets. They start looking at each other without value. For them, it seems like it's so easy to kill people. I don't know where all that anger is coming from. I know they have it hard, but why are they doing bad things to each other?

Q: Your answer is similar to the reasons given for the recent school violence— the feeling of being "outsiders."

A: When you're young—I'm not that old—when you're young, you feel you don't have any options. You can't see that far ahead, and when you're black, you don't even see the next day. You live for this moment, for this hour; you don't see a future. You see people dying for nothing. My brother could have died because someone wanted the chain around his neck, or my other brother could have died because he was "messing" with the wrong girl. When you feel these thoughts, or recognize the problems in society, life becomes hopeless. And if you can't look ahead, or inside of yourself to know the potential, you get lost, you get lost in the shuffle. And that's what happens to a lot of brothers.

Q: What makes you different—did any members of your peer group influence you?

A: When I was in high school, I was always a leader. I've always been my own individual, so I didn't really look for anyone to follow. My peers didn't influence me; I admired some of my peers who were able to achieve academically or artistically, but I never wanted to fashion myself after anyone, not any of my peers. I was mainly influenced by some of the material that I read, and I was mainly influenced by not wanting to become a victim, and I know that's what pushed me: I didn't want to fail. I really can't say any one individual influenced me.

Q: Have any of your teachers influenced you?

A: When I was in high school, I would have to say, "No." When I was in junior high school, I had a teacher, Ms. L. in the eighth grade, my English teacher, and she influenced me. I wanted to excel in academics, and she reinforced me. She was like a personal cheerleader. She would say, "Oh you are doing so well!" In that way, she influenced me a lot. In high school, my tenth grade English teacher influenced my life. She taught me subjects inside the classroom, and she also taught me how to be successful, to be black and successful outside the classroom. She is still a friend of mine. I listened and learned. I consider myself a good listener; it is the easiest way to learn.

Observer's Comments about Respondent

- her greatest obstacle has been "violence," especially the murders of her two brothers;
- is serious and analytical;
- realizes she has to map out a future for herself;
- is a dedicated student;
- feels her father has taken no role in family life.

INTERVIEW 6

Q: What factors do you identify as contributing to your success?
A: I would have to say my mother and my grandmother. My grandmother dropped out of high school, but she went back and got her high school diploma as well as her bachelor's degree. My mother also got her bachelor's degree. My mother and my grandmother actually graduated college at the same time. It was very nice to see that—inspiring for me.

Q: Are they your role models?
A: Yes, they are.

Q: Who brought you up?
A: My mother, my mother.

Q: Does your father live at your home?
A: No, my father never did; he was never there.

Q: Can you tell us a little bit about your father?
A: I don't know him, never met him, so I don't have any idea of his character at all.

Q: Did your mother ever tell you about your father?
A: There was a male figure in my life that was constant, and I believed him to be my father. In my eyes, he was my father; I loved him, but it wasn't until I was sixteen that my mother explained to me that he wasn't my father. She didn't go into detail about my biological father, and I didn't ask her. I really wasn't concerned; I was just happy knowing the man that I knew. It wasn't very important to me.

Q: Do you miss not having your father in the house?
A: No. I don't regret my upbringing. I didn't want for anything, and actually, the man that I thought was my father gave me everything I needed and the majority of the things that I wanted, so I didn't know there was something missing in the home.

Q: What factors do you identify as obstacles that you had to overcome in order to reach this status [college] in your life?
A: I don't know if there were really any obstacles; there was a point where I felt that maybe I wasn't in college for myself. Maybe it was because I was

expected to follow in somebody's footsteps. I took one year off from school, but that one year was enough time for me to realize that I needed an education. There was nothing out there that really attracted me, and I knew that I wanted to become a teacher, so I came back to school. I know the importance of a college degree.

Q: What determining factor motivated you toward teaching as a goal?
A: I love kids, and I love interacting with them. I love being able to just learn from them, and, hopefully, they'll learn from me. I like the interaction when we're connecting and drawing from each other; so it's just a love—my calling.

Q: What grade levels are you preparing to teach?
A: I want to teach ninth grade through twelfth grade.

Q: Isn't that the most difficult age group?
A: No. Middle school would be considered the difficult age group to teach. I wouldn't mind teaching middle school, but my heart is at the senior high school level.

Q: What is your major field of study?
A: English education.

Q: What courses of action would you take if you had to overcome a difficult obstacle in your life?
A: I would probably step away from the problem and view it from a little distance, and then figure out the best way to overcome it. It depends on the situation, of course, and it depends on how bad I want to overcome that obstacle. Is it something I can dismiss from my life, or is it something that I want to overcome? If it is something that I know I have to conquer, I will become determined.

Q: What thoughts pass through your mind when making a decision?
A: What would be the best outcome—for me and the people involved? Mostly, what is the best outcome for all?

Q: Is the church a major influence in your life?
A: Oh, very much so. My grandmother is the pastor of my church, and my mother is the assistant pastor, so I grew up in the church. I admit, once I left home, I fell away from it, because that point in life was of discovery for me. Religion wasn't forced on me, but I have a strong religious background.

Q: What is the most significant result of your strong religious background?
A: Gaining a sense of values and strong sense of morals so that I won't disrespect myself. Also, my respect for others.

Q: Do you know any young women who have had children out of wedlock?
A: Yes, I do.

Q: Why do young women have babies out of wedlock?
A: I think each woman has a different situation, a different predicament. Some of the girls may be too young to think ahead, to know the probable consequences; some young women are carried away by strong emotion, and they think their strong emotion and their boyfriend's strong emotion will end up in an ongoing relationship. I really don't have an opinion on kids having kids. It is an individual crisis.

Q: How do these women survive after having a child out of wedlock—where do they go from there?
A: Nowhere. It messes up their lives. Grandmothers don't want to take care of their children's children. Today, the grandmother is young and has her own life, her own career. Mothers need to educate their daughters on the true facts of life—that only when you make good decisions will you have a positive life. If you don't put the best into it, make good choices, life will hit you head-on. This is a new millenium. Mothers need to educate their daughters on the true facts of life.

Observer's Comment about Respondent

- hesitates when asked about her father;
- mother and grandmother are her role models;
- is quiet and reserved.

INTERVIEW 8

Q: What factors do you identify as contributing to your success?
A: The first factor is my mother. She instilled proper behavior. The second factor is my church. My mother and grandmother instilled the importance of attending church.

Q: Why is attending church a major factor?
A: Attending church helps young people because [of] the many activities that church offers, which helps keep them off the streets. I was a member of the youth choir and the bugle corps in the marching band. I was also active in Sunday school, which my mother participated in, and I also learned leadership ability from my church.

Q: How does that help you today?
A: I am very far from home. Therefore, I have to be responsible for myself. Being aware of leadership responsibility has helped me to know what I am supposed to do and what I am not supposed to do. Because of my upbringing, I am able to make the right decisions and stay out of trouble. I don't get involved in anything that will lead to trouble.

Q: What factors do you identify as obstacles?
A: At this time, I do not have any obstacles in my life. My mother and grandmother are always looking out for me. If I have any problems, I call home.

Q: Who (what) are your models?
A: My models are my mother, grandmother, and the teachings of the church. They are basically the influences in my life.

Q: How did your mother serve as a role model?
A: My mother taught me how to be a young lady, what to do and what not to do. I also observed my mother as a single parent. I always knew my father, but I didn't live with him. There was no child support, because my mother didn't insist on child support from my father. My mother wanted to raise me on her own, but my father did assist in my upbringing. But most of the upbringing came from my mom, who taught me how to be strong. She is a very strong woman.

Q: Did your mother ever marry?
A: No, my mother never married.

Q: How old was your mother when she gave birth to you?
A: My mother was twenty-five years old when she had me.

Q: What was your grandmother's role in your life?
A: When I was younger, my mother used to live with my grandmother. Basically, my grandmother was around 50 percent of the time. My mom and grandmother brought me up equally. Both of them have been my parents.

Q: How old is your grandmother?
A: I think my grandmother is seventy-two years old. People in my family live to be pretty old.

Q: Did you miss not having a father in the home?
A: No, because he lived close by. My father lived in Maryland, which is only fifteen minutes away from where I grew up in Washington, D.C. I actually liked it, because I got double Christmas presents and double birthday presents. I was spoiled, because I am my mother's only child. It did not really bother me or matter much to me. I do not think it would have made much difference in my life.

Q: Did he [your father] represent someone whom you could emulate?
A: Yes, my father is a role model, but I don't relate to him as such, because he is a male. I am used to my mother; she taught me how to become a woman. But, my father teaches me not to look down on anyone and to help people. He is very helpful; he owns a towing company. Sometimes [he meets] homeless people [looking] for a place to stay and he sets out a van for them. He allows them to stay there until they get on their feet. In that sense, my father is a role model; he is a good person.

Q: Did your mother ever discuss her teenage pregnancy with you?
A: My mother never discussed personal matters like that with me. However, she did tell me about my father and their relationship when they were dating.

But she only discussed minor issues with me, not any large issues. I know she was a young parent still living with my grandmother when she got pregnant. The only minus was the fact that she never married. But she does not consider me a mistake.

Q: Why do you think young women have children out of wedlock?
A: I think it could be for many reasons. In high school, I think many of the young ladies try to fit in with the crowd by wearing makeup and revealing clothes. Sometimes, the guys are just smooth with the girls. It depends on one's upbringing, mind set, and teachings. Young women need to learn about men through their brothers or fathers. If they don't have either, it is just a guessing game. Personally, I do not want to be a statistic. Basically, I guess it is just the mind-set. Many of the young women sneak around and do what they want to do, regardless of rules—particularly dorm rules. Behavior such as this eventually catches up to them, and the women get pregnant.

Q: Are you saying the girls sneak the guys into the dormitory?
A: I do not know if they sneak guys in anymore; cameras are set up now. However, in 1996 and 1997 there was a huge baby boom. Those were the same people that were sneaking out, but I guess it's all in the upbringing. Sometimes, the girls have more than one partner. They really [do] not think.

Q: Do you know any of the girls that got pregnant at that time and what they are doing presently?
A: Yes, I know a few people who got pregnant in 1996. Most of them went back home to get help with the baby; most of the guys are not with them, anymore.

Q: Do these young women ever return to college?
A: Most of the women who leave college say that they are going to take a break for at least a year, but some never return. Some come back three or four years later. If I was to get pregnant, knowing that I come from a certain type of family, and with God's help, I would be able to return to school. I would probably go home, have the baby, then return to school. I would also have my mother move in with me. But I would not get pregnant from someone who would not take the responsibilities that come with having a baby. In reality, I am not ready to take on that responsibility, anyway. Without a college education, what would I do for work? The girls that got themselves into that situation should have known better; most of them did not have jobs either.

Q: Did your mother have a college education?
A: My mother went to business school; when she completed high school, she was not interested in college, but she graduated from business school.

Q: What type of work does your mother do?
A: My mother is an administrative assistant to a senator in Washington.

Q: How long has your mother held that position?
A: She has been in that position for about six months. She has very high goals, and her dream has always been to go right to the top. She wanted to start her own business in transcribing, but that didn't work out for her. She had to get a new job, and she got the job as assistant to a senator.

Q: What passes through your mind when making a decision?
A: I think about my ROTC [Reserve Officers' Training Corps] instructor in high school. In ninth grade, he would get us involved in the decision making processes, and I think about that sometimes. I also think about my mother and grandmother.

Q: What is the key to the decision-making process?
A: The key to the decision-making process is to sift everything through—sift ideas through a web-like formation. Make a web and put little arrows through the spaces or lines of the web to signify the pros and cons. When it is a real tough decision, I . . . think about that process.

Q: Describe the home that you grew up in.
A: The home I grew up in was church-oriented. My family is very religious; however, they are not perfect. They are bold; they tell family members what they think, whether the person wants to hear it or not. They would make their feelings known. They have always tried to make me think of my future, and to make me think about accomplishments, and they let me know it. It is very important to them; it has become very important to me.

Q: How do you define success?
A: Success can be defined as acquiring knowledge. I believe that attaining an education creates a better life and success. Many people start college and then stop, but I want to keep pursuing an education. Changes in society happen every day. For example, computers are being updated on a daily basis, and learning becomes a necessary part of life—a necessity, a lifelong challenge.

Q: What recommendations do you have for younger black women in the community?
A: I would encourage them to think about their dreams and go after them. Regardless how hard it seems, go for it. That is my recommendation for younger black women in the community.

Q: Have you experienced any violence in school or in the community?
A: It would probably be a high school fight. I have never seen any serious violence or anyone get killed. I have been sheltered by my parents. They try to keep me away from harm.

Q: Presently, we have unprecedented violence in schools and in the community. Do you have any thoughts about why that happens?
A: Young people feel that they have to fit in, and they get caught up with the wrong crowd. Gang-related clashes are brainless; yet they exist. High schools

breed violence with other high schools. They compete in sports, group against group. Anger also breaks out between two sets of students in the same school, because they are in different groups. I would say, it is because they are not listened to, or understood. Most of the time, they are just being mean. I do not think metal detectors will help. I believe that prayer should be [allowed] in schools. When prayer was taken out of schools, it opened up opportunities for trouble. I know that some people do not have the same beliefs, but prayer should be a part of the school day. If a person does not believe in prayer, then he or she should not be made to participate, but as long as prayer is acknowledged, there will be room for change.

Q: Do you feel that violence stems from feelings of being an outsider?
A: Yes, I feel that is a major part of the problem, and, sometimes, it is the fault of the parent. If you cannot respect your mom, or home, then you will not respect the teachers, or the facilities. If you do not respect the person who gave birth to you, I do not think you know what respect is all about.

Q: Are there any other thoughts that you wish to share with young people in the community?
A: Learn a bit more of your city; learn a bit more of the world. My mom had a lot to do with that, also. When I was in high school, I went to a rough high school, but I was never a part of the bad set. I was in the gospel and show choirs. Our teacher, Miss H., helped us get through problem times. In June 1996, we went to Paris and sang for two weeks. Before then, I had a counselor who made it possible for me to go to Russia for a month. My advice is, even though the schools might be rough and dangerous, find the good; there is always some good to discover. My school was dangerous to the point where we had metal detectors; yet someone got shot inside the school. With all of that, there are still little opportunities to explore, if you look close enough. You have to take advantage of the good—that could get you set for the future.

Q: Are you emphasizing that school activities, like joining the choir, helped you get through troublesome times in high school?
A: Yes, I would say the choirs helped a lot. When I first got to high school, I didn't want to join, but I joined because I like to sing. Miss H., the instructor, understood her students. If we had problems, we could always talk to her. She cared about us very much—her caring helped me get through.

Q: Do you feel a connection between the historical experiences of blacks and whites in America and the present disconnect between blacks and whites in America?
A: I feel that we should look at a person for who they are, not for the color of that person. I have not had any problems, but I have a lot of friends who actually despise white people; I cannot agree with that. I have known many white people who helped me in my jobs and school work. People help people. It is not all about color or race. I do not think we should focus on that.

Observer's Comments about Respondent

- sensible;
- confident;
- positive.

INTERVIEW 9

Q: What factors do you identify as contributing to your success?
A: The most important factor is the time that I spend studying.

Q: What major obstacles did you have to overcome to come to college?
A: The major obstacles were many: lack of money, personal matters, and the decision to leave my mom, who was sick. Another problem was that I had to go to court. A guy ran into my house when he was running from the cops. I was home alone. We pressed charges, and I had to go to court. It is a wonder that I finally made it to college.

Q: Can you describe the neighborhood that you lived in while growing up?
A: My neighborhood had drug dealers hanging out on the corners and crime was frequent; crime was very frequent. There were many people who got shot; my brother got shot. There were a lot of young kids dealing drugs; it seemed like they didn't have anything better to do. My neighborhood could be a decent one, but most of the neighbors do not stick together as a community, and they don't put down rules. The kids were painting "garbage" all over the walls and street signs, and the neighbors would not get together as a community and complain.

Q: What was your mother's reaction to all of this?
A: My mother was the type who did not tolerate bad behavior, and she would tell the kids to get out of the yard and go down the block. They did bad things right in front of our house, and a lot of young kids did not want to listen. I feel my neighborhood was full of young kids, who did not have anything to do, so they just decided that they would do mischief, and they did.

Q: How old were the children?
A: The children were young; most of them were in middle school. They were between the ages of thirteen and sixteen.

Q: What kind of families did they come from?
A: I do not think that their parents trained them like my mom trained me. There were a lot of homes where the father was not present; the kids did not want to listen. They were mostly guys who did not want to listen.

Q: Did you live in the inner city?
A: Yes, I lived in the inner city; I lived in Atlanta; the population was black. Now, I live in Melbourne, Florida, which is a medium-size community.

Q: How long have you lived in Melbourne?
A: I came to Melbourne when I was nine years old; I have been there for a long time; I am twenty-one now.

Q: What was the worst episode that you experienced living in the inner city?
A: My brother's best friend, and many others, got shot. Those experiences were a nightmare.

Q: Why did he get shot?
A: A silly reason. A fight in my brother's car, and my brother's friend broke up the fight. During the fight, one of the guys hit his head on the car door, and the guy was mad about that. When it was all over, my brother's friend started to go home; the same guy drove up behind him, turned off the lights of his car, and shot. After he got shot, he was trying to run home; his house was right across the street from ours. But he didn't survive; he died in the middle of the street.

Q: How old was he?
A: He was close in age to us; he had to be twenty-two or twenty-three.

Q: Why do young people resort to violence and guns so often now?
A: Years ago, young people fought it out with their hands. Now, young people think that they are taking the easy way out by settling a fight with a gun. They just want to shoot.

Q: Did the police ever find the person who shot your brother's friend?
A: Yes, they found him; I believe he turned himself in.

Q: What was his penalty?
A: I am not sure, but I know that he is still in jail.

Q: What is the cause of rage among young people?
A: They feel that they are misunderstood, and not being heard by anyone. They probably feel that when they use a gun they will get instant attention. They also have no respect for authority. They feel that they have nothing to lose, because they are down and out right now and nobody seems to care. It does not really matter to them if they use violence, if they kill somebody, or if they go to jail. The younger ones know that they are not going to get the death penalty, because they are not [yet] eighteen. They also know that they are going to get right back out after a certain period of time.

Q: Is it a cry for help or a suicide attempt on their part?
A: I do not think it is that at all, because those kids have friends and family. I think it has to do with peer pressure. I do not think it is a cry for help.

Q: Do you feel fear in your neighborhood?
A: It was like that for a while, and my mother and I were fed up. We were angry, and we felt resentment to have to put up with feelings of fear in our

own neighborhood. Most of these kids I knew; I grew up with them and went to school with them. I went to junior high school with them and that is probably as far as some of them went. I do not feel fear anymore, because after the guy came into our house, I agreed to go to court to testify against him. He knew I was going to testify. I am just fed up now, and so is my mother. My mother is the last person to fear those kids; she would say to them, "Would you please get out of my yard?" I do not know if she says "please" anymore, but I do not think that I should have to be afraid to step outside my door.

Q: Was the man who came into your house the same person who shot and killed your brother's friend?
A: Oh no, that was not the same guy. I do not even know the guy who came into the house.

Q: Why did the man come into your house?
A: The guy that came into our house was running from the police. The kids in my neighborhood are out on the corner all the time, and when they see a cop, they all start running. I ran out of the house when he ran in, because I didn't know him. I saw a police officer, who was in ordinary clothes, and I told him that the guy was in my house. He went into the house, and I ran across the street. Now, the guys know that I will testify against them, if I have to.

Q: Who brought you up?
A: I was the youngest in my house. I have a sister and a brother, who watched out for me, but, mainly, my mother watched out for me.

Q: Have you communicated with your father?
A: I was too young to remember anything about my father. When I was about six, my mom left him. My father was in jail from when I was six years old, and I did not remember him at all. When I became eighteen, I decided that I wanted to meet him, and I drove with two friends to the Georgia state prison. There, I met my father. I was just curious, and I wanted to know. My mom never really told me anything about my father, because she thought it was in my best interest that I should not know these things. My father did evil things, and my mom just never told me. My father and I kept in touch by talking on the phone a couple of times a week after I met him in jail, but, at that time, I did not know why he was in jail. I eventually figured it out by bits and pieces, because my mom gave me some papers to read and I read what happened— basically, why he was in jail. When I found out, it was too much for me, and I could see why my mother didn't tell me—now, I understand that. I do not know if I forgave him, or if I accepted those things that he did, but a year after that, I just stopped writing him. I am in college, and he doesn't know that I am here.

Q: What were your feelings about not having a father in the home while you were growing up?

A: Sometimes, I wonder if I had a father in the home if anything would have been different, but I am not saying that things would have been better if I had a father in the home. At this point, all I have is my mother, and that is all I need. As far as my brother, I think things would have been different for him if our father were there, but I do not feel that I really missed out on anything. I just wish . . . but I have my brother, and he took the place of my father. I do not feel that I missed out on anything.

Q: How old is your brother now?
A: My brother is twenty-five years old, and he has three kids. I guess he is doing the best he can right now in his situation.

Q: What does he do for a living?
A: He was in school, and I do not know if he is working right now. At this time, he is taking care of the baby, who will be one year old in two weeks.

Q: Does his wife work?
A: She is a manager at a restaurant; they are not married.

Q: Do you think that black men have a more difficult time getting work than black women?
A: One of the reasons that my brother can't find work is that he was arrested and spent the night in jail. When prospective employers [learn] that, they do not hire him; it is really hard. Also, I do not know if he is applying himself the way he should. At first, I thought these guys [black men like my brother] were just being lazy, but, to be honest, they really have a hard time. When [employers see] a black male, they think he will fail; sometimes [black males do fail,] and sometimes they don't. But they expect black males to fail; the employers are always waiting for something to happen, and they are constantly on their backs about everything. It is hard, and guys have to deal with that, and, then, they have to come home and deal with their wife or girlfriend. It is hard, and I understand, but I do not think the black [males] should make excuses. I think that they should apply themselves as much as they can. It is also difficult for women to get a job, because there is competition with other people wanting the same job. If you do not have an education, or a degree, then it is even harder. True, it was harder for some black men, but when affirmative action came around, then it was not that hard anymore. But I do think women get jobs easier, even if it is only a cashier's job. I think women get jobs before the guys.

Q: Are you involved in the church?
A: My mom never made us get up and go to church, because, she felt, if that was something we wanted to do, then we would do that on our own. Religion is not something that you can force on someone; it is a personal relationship with your God. You should find your own way—that is the way my mother brought us up. She did not force us to go to church. When I was growing up,

I went to church, but I made that choice; now that I am in college, it feels like something I have to do. When I do not go home on the weekends, I go to the school chapel on Sundays.

Q: Did your peers influence you in any way?
A: No, kids my age did things that they were not supposed to do, and what I was not supposed to do. They only influenced me to better myself, because when I looked at what they were doing, I knew I did not want to do that. I am twenty-one years old, living in the freshmen dorms, with seventeen- and eighteen-year-old girls, who want to drink and smoke, and also do other things they have no business doing. I am not going to act like them; they have not influenced me to do negative things. I look at them, and they remind me of what not to do. They only influenced me in that way. I learn from them what not to do.

Q: What thoughts go through your mind when you have to make a decision?
A: It all depends on what I have to decide; I always think about the consequences for me and my family. My family comes first.

Q: Who is your role model?
A: My mother is my role model, and I look at her as my hero. She accomplished so much that I thought [was] impossible. She taught me how to be independent, how to do things for myself, and not to rely on a man.

Q: Can you give us a picture of your mother's life?
A: She raised three kids by herself, and she worked. My mother worked and worked. She is still working to this day. She would work night jobs and day jobs. My mother did whatever she had to do to make sure we had shoes on our feet and food to eat. Everything she did was for us—makes her a good mother.

Q: Do you see a difference in young mothers today?
A: Some women nowadays do not take care of their kids the way that they should. These girls are young and having kids. Their mentality is way off. There were times when my mother did not have new clothes, but we did. She would sacrifice so much for us. Now, young girls that have babies are selfish. They don't sacrifice for their children. They want new clothes, manicured nails—while their kids have dirty faces and snotty noses. I do not understand, because my mother would sacrifice for us. Today, many women would not sacrifice like my mother did. My mother is a superwoman type to me.

Q: What kind of work does she do?
A: She works in a hospital. She gets the birth certificates and social security numbers for newborn babies.

Q: Was your grandmother involved in bringing you up?
A: I do not remember anything about my grandmother. I know we are living in her house now, and my mom had to take care of her because she was sick. I think she died when I was nine years old, or younger.

Q: Were you involved in athletics when you were growing up?
A: Yes, I was a tomboy; I would get into everything. I was not committed to anything special, but I was very active. I would play tennis, volleyball, and basketball. I tried out for the basketball team in junior high, and I was the first one to get chosen. Then I made the team again, but I had to stop when my brother was in the hospital.

Q: Are you participating in any athletics in college?
A: No, I am not, because I went to a community college, and sports activities don't exist. When I came here, I did want to play football, but I didn't have the time.

Q: Are you involved in organizations at the college?
A: I am involved in the prealumni counsel. It is an organization that promotes the United Negro College Fund; we go to regional and national conferences to represent the college. We also raise funds.

Q: When you were growing up, were you active in the community?
A: I was a candy striper; I volunteered in high school. I was not involved in any high school clubs, because I wanted to come home and watch cartoons. I just wanted to run home and play with my sister.

Q: What is your sister doing now?
A: My sister also works in the hospital.

Q: In what capacity?
A: My sister works in out-patient registration.

Q: Does she have a college education?
A: My sister went to the same community college that I went to, but she did not finish her course work. She wanted to work in the medical field, but discovered that she didn't like it. I had tried to encourage her to go back to college and take business courses. I will eventually get her to go back to school. At this time, she is working, but she doesn't like her job.

Q: Is she older than you?
A: We are six years apart; I am twenty-one, and she is twenty-seven.

Q: What is inside you that motivates you to succeed?
A: I do not want to disappoint my family; I want to get my degree and make my mom proud. She is the only reason why I am here. She is my motivation. My nephew asks me about college and that also encourages me to go. I want to finish college so that my family will be proud of me. I also know that I need to have a degree if I want to succeed.

Q: What are your goals?
A: I have short- and long-term goals. A short-term goal may be finishing a research paper on the due date; a long-term goal would be getting my college degree. I always make short- and long-term goals.

Q: How do you define success?
A: Success is different for different people. Little successes can mean that you have completed your immediate goal. Success for some people can mean having a house, a car, and enough money to pay the bills. When you accomplish your set goal—that is success.

Q: What do you think is going to happen to those kids who spend so much time on the street and get involved in criminal activity?
A: What I think is going to happen has already happened. Most of them are dead or in jail.

Q: Do you think that race prejudice plays a part in their downfall?
A: In my mind, if they are using that as an explanation, it is only an excuse. I know the color of my skin will not prevent me from getting a job or a raise. I think it is only an excuse. I do not think that plays a part in their fate.

Q: Do you think their environment influences them, and they just succumb?
A: Yes, I believe it is peer pressure. Some of them get into gangs and sell drugs. Some girls get caught up with guys and get pregnant. I think it has a lot to do with the environment. I have come this far, and I am not going to allow that to happen to me. I have seen a lot of disturbing things happen, but I am not going to get caught up in it. Going to church has helped me not to get caught up. I believe that if you know about the Bible, or believe in God, you will not get into those negative activities.

Q: Can you explain why young girls have sexual relations, do not protect themselves, and get pregnant at such a young age?
A: They probably know better, but they are probably curious. Mostly, they do not care. Most of the girls know what could happen. In my neighborhood, girls were having kids at twelve and thirteen years old.

Q: Who takes care of the babies?
A: Their moms take care of the babies to a certain point. The fathers probably give money to help buy diapers. The girls would take care of them to a certain extent, by making sure they had a pair of Nikes [sneakers] or a new outfit, but they do not teach them morals. The mom does not have any type of morals to pass down to the kids.

Q: How do you teach responsibility to those girls who lack responsibility; how do you get them to think?
A: The hardest thing to do is to tell someone who is not responsible that they should change their behavior and attitudes. They do not want to listen, and they have no respect for authority or their elders. At this time, my roommate is behaving badly, and I cannot tell her what she is doing is not appropriate. It is difficult to tell someone they are taking the wrong path. Eventually, they will figure it out themselves.

Q: Who do they follow?

A: It is peer pressure right now, and they just follow other students. They are eighteen years old, fresh out of high school, and the first time out of the house. The girls don't know what they are doing is wrong. There are so many subjects that I would like to discuss with my roommate. I would like to tell her that if she is going with these guys, just to be careful.

Q: What is the future for these young women, particularly those who have children out of wedlock? What is a realistic outcome for them?

A: To be honest, I cannot speak for everybody, but when my mother had me, she wasn't married; she had three kids with the same man. Then, to think about worse situations, some women have kids by different fathers. There is no excuse for these women. Fortunately, my mother kept her mind on us, because we were her responsibility.

Q: What recommendations do you have for younger black women in the community?

A: I am young myself, and I am always open to advice from an older woman. I am always willing to listen and learn. I think other girls really need to listen and learn. I would say that when your mom, aunt, or teacher gives advice, you should listen, because they have been there.

Q: Do these young women prefer to experiment with life on their own instead of listening?

A: I think so. They are curious, and they want to know. Eventually, the mother would have to let them go. I was the youngest, and my mom had me by the neck. She only let me go when I went to college. I am glad she didn't let me go earlier, because if she did, I probably would be like my roommate; I probably would get pregnant like the other girls.

Q: Are you saying that your mother was very strict?

A: Yes, my mother was very strict and for good reasons.

Q: Did you fear her strictness?

A: Yes, if I did something wrong, I knew I was going to get it. She would discipline us by spanking us and not allowing us to go outside to play. I feared getting spanked.

Q: Is your mother your role model?

A: Yes, my mother and my elementary school principal, Mr. T. He turned me around. In school, I had a temper and bad grades, and he turned my life around. I got kicked out of elementary school because I was so bad. In elementary school, I would beat up other kids and hit my teachers. I didn't know what was wrong with me, and my mom didn't know what was wrong with me. I had just moved to Florida. I was sent to a special school for children with disabilities. They put me in a class with those kinds of kids, and I would be in the principal's office about twice a day.

Q: Why, and what happened?

A: The first year the principal knew me by my name. Sometimes, he would come and get me out of class. He would get on the phone and call my mom, and she [would know] I had done something wrong again. She would give him permission to paddle me, and he broke a paddle on me once. He had four different paddles on his shelf, and I knew the procedure. I bent over on the desk, and he paddled me hard. That man turn me around; I did not want to get paddled anymore, and I think the last time was when he broke that paddle on me. That was the last time I went to his office for being bad. After that, I would only go to his office to get the principal's award or because I made the honor role. That man turned me around, and I made straight As. He was here for homecoming, and I believe he went to school here, but I am not sure. I think he and my mother ganged up on me and turned me around.

Q: Do you believe in strict discipline and hard punishment for children who are difficult?

A: It worked for me; I know it did.

Observer's Comments about Respondent

- physically strong;
- strong motivation;
- says she "looks like dad";
- but "acts like mom."

INTERVIEW 10

Q: What factors contribute to your success?

A: My mother.

Q: In what way did she contribute?

A: She said, "You're going to college, and you don't have a choice."

Q: Did your parents attend college?

A: Both went to college.

Q: Was your father involved in your upbringing?

A: He was involved, but my mom basically ran the show.

Q: In what way?

A: She always had to know the name of the person that I was talking with on the telephone, where I was going, and the time that I was returning; on the other hand, my father was always the person whom I could plead to when my mother said, "No!"

Q: In what way did your father help you?

A: He was more like a friend than a dad. He was the reason that I love football and basketball. I was the first child, and they thought I would be a boy. He did not have his son, so I became the substitute son. We were always friends rather than father and daughter.

Q: Are your parents married now?
A: No; they recently split up.

Q: Was that a major problem for you?
A: Not for me, but probably for my sister and my brother. At the time, I was already out of the house, so it didn't really make a difference to me.

Q: What is your life like presently—do you have a child?
A: Yes.

Q: When you had the child were you married?
A: No.

Q: How old is the child now?
A: She will be three in April.

Q: Who helps you to take care of the child when you are in school and at work?
A: She goes to day care during the day, and, then, her dad picks her up when he gets off from work at 5:00 P.M., and they're home together. I leave school at 7:30 P.M. every night.

Q: Are you living with the father of your child?
A: Yes, we live together.

Q: Do you plan to marry him?
A: Yes.

Q: When are you going to get married?
A: Sometime this year, but I don't know yet.

Q: Which one of you hesitates to marry?
A: I think it is me.

Q: Why?
A: I really want a wedding, but I don't have time to plan it. I need to graduate college; that is the first priority right now; then, I'll have time to plan a wedding the way I want it.

Q: Is your boyfriend in college now?
A: No. He already graduated from college—Florida Memorial College.

Q: What does he do for a living?
A: He works in an accounting firm in Fort Lauderdale.

Q: How does he get involved in [his daughter's] care? Does he discipline her?

A: He just leaves that all to me. He can't stand to see her cry. She is three years old now, and I don't think she should have her own way, but she gets everything she wants from her dad.

Q: How do you discipline her?
A: She gets a couple of spanks now and then; she is at a precocious age—nothing major—but she is two handsful.

Q: When she was born who took care of her?
A: I did. I was not in school at the time.

Q: Who were you living with?
A: My parents—in their home.

Q: When you told them that you were pregnant, what was their reaction?
A: They were not happy, but I was twenty-one years old and considered an adult.

Q: Do they enjoy their grandchild?
A: Yes, they really do.

Q: From your perspective, what are the reasons for very young girls having children out of wedlock?
A: They are trying to be adults at fourteen years old, but the reality is that they cannot accept the responsibilities of adulthood. But fourteen year old children get pregnant and have children; yet, they are children themselves. Families, and eventually society, have the burden of "children having children," the child-mother, who can't take care of herself yet.

Q: What about the young men in these circumstances?
A: The majority of the time, the guys are not ready to be fathers. The older generation was not that different. My grandmother got pregnant when she was sixteen; eventually, she married my grandfather, and they stayed together until my grandfather died.

Q: Did your grandmother admonish you about getting pregnant without being married?
A: My grandmother didn't, because I didn't tell her for a long time. When she did know, and when my mother would get angry at me, my grandmother would tell her not to, because she understood. My grandmother was even younger than I was when she became pregnant. Because of her own experience, she understood how afraid I really was.

Q: Was your mother married when she had you?
A: Yes.

Q: Are you involved in extracurricular activities in college?
A: I am not. I go to class, then I go home.

Q: When you were growing up, what did you experience as obstacles to overcome?
A: I don't think I really had any obstacles. I never had a difficult time in school, except for math and science.

Q: When you were growing up, were you involved in school activities?
A: Yes, I was in the school band; I also ran track and participated in club activities.

Q: What activity did you enjoy the most?
A: In the tenth, eleventh, and twelfth grade, I was a dancer with the school band. I had fun; we went on trips; my friends now are the same ones that I met through the band activities.

Q: If you had a choice to do something over in your life what would that be?
A: I think I would have stayed in Tennessee, where I previously attended school. I think I was homesick, and it was cold, but I know I would have graduated college many years ago if I had stayed.

Q: Do you plan to go to graduate school?
A: I plan to take at least two years off, then go back to school, so yes, but I am not sure about the field that I will study.

Q: Did you get a good education in the public school system in Dade County [Florida]?
A: Yes, I think so.

Q: Did you witness any violence in the neighborhood that you grew up in?
A: I witnessed some at school, but not in my neighborhood. I went to American High School in Hialeah, and I lived in Carol City. But we did have fights. I also experienced young people shooting guns at parties, but not in my neighborhood; I can't say that I did.

Q: What causes young people to get into conflicts at school?
A: Kids don't know how to deal with their anger. They interpret students' behavior as belittling them. Their reactions of frustration and anger boil over to violence and killing. I don't think they realize that death is permanent—that when you kill somebody, you end your own life, too—that they will spend the rest of their life in jail. The law in Florida is clear—the ten to 20 to life law. If you pull a gun, you get ten years in jail, and if you fire a gun, you get twenty years. If you hit someone, you get a life sentence. Young people have to learn how to deal with their anger.

Q: Are the young people aware of the law?
A: I hear it on the radio everyday, so I am sure they are aware. If one of their friends [was] put in jail, they might take more notice.

Q: Can you give us an example of conflicts that you have experienced?

A: On one occasion, a girl was dancing with a guy at a party, and her boyfriend came in. He became angry, went to his car, and got a gun; we all had to run and leave the party.

Q: Did he shoot?
A: Yes, he shot, but no one got hurt.

Q: What were the consequences?
A: I don't know. It happened on the night of my high school graduation, and I got out of there fast.

Q: When you were growing up, were you involved in church activities?
A: Yes; I spent most of my days in church. We attended church all day Sunday, Bible study on Monday night, choir rehearsal on Wednesday night, but I eventually got tired of the church. I haven't gone lately, but I am trying to get involved again.

Q: Were most of the folks attending church women?
A: Yes, old women.

Q: Why is the church so important to the older women in the black community?
A: Going to church becomes a lifelong habit. It is also a social gathering; for instance, my grandmother and all her friends meet at church.

Q: Were your grandparents involved in your upbringing?
A: Neither of my grandfathers were involved in my upbringing; my mother's parents are divorced. My [maternal] grandfather moved out of state (from Florida to New York), but I know my grandmothers very well.

Q: Did your grandmothers influence you?
A: My father's mother lectured me daily about saving money, because I love to shop. My other grandmother died last year; she was always sick.

Q: Do you think that grandmothers bring the family together?
A: I believe that they do.

Q: In retrospect, would you [prefer to] have waited to get pregnant?
A: Yes, I would have finished college first; I would have been teaching for a year now.

Q: What is your major goal?
A: I want to become an English teacher

Q: What advice would you give young black women in the community?
A: I would tell them that they definitely need an education. Their main goal should be to enter and stay in college until they get a degree. Not to depend on someone supporting them the rest of their life. Just depend on yourself. Getting an education is the first factor in getting ahead in the best way possible—in the safest way possible.

Observer's Comments about Respondent

- is always in a hurry;
- takes on too many tasks;
- interned at a local high school;
- loves teaching.

INTERVIEW 12

Q: What factors do you identify as contributing to your success?
A: The factor that I identity as contributing to my success is my strong family background. My parents motivated me to succeed by encouraging me to go to college and get a good education.

Q: How many children are in your family? Would you explain [the] roles within the family group?
A: There are four children in the family, and I am child number three. My mother's role is dominant in the home. My father tries to be the financial provider for the family, and basically, he is the sole supporter of the household.

Q: Did your father give you any parental guidance?
A: My father instilled rules for me to follow. He encouraged me to be a strong person within myself, even though people made fun of me sometimes. I always heard negative remarks from others, but he always stressed that I be a strong women and stand on my own two feet.

Q: What kind of negative remarks would you hear from others?
A: The negative remarks were that I would never succeed, and I would never get into college. I was often told that I was not smart enough to get into college. Those kind of remarks made me question myself. Then, I would doubt myself.

Q: What relationship did you or your family have with those people?
A: Friends of my parents told [my mom] that they [did] not think that her children were going to accomplish anything in life, and I had friends that told me the same thing.

Q: Why would someone say something like that?
A: My parents only finished high school; they did not attend college. They only picked up trades, and these people thought that we were going to follow in their footsteps and have a hard life.

Q: What is your mother's role in the family?
A: My mother's role is the dominant figure and what she says in the home basically goes. She controls the finances, by determining how much we need to save and spend. My mother plays the major, dominant role in the home.

Q: Do your mother and father have good communication between them?
A: My parents have excellent communication between them. We have a spiritual family, and I have grown up in the church. According to my father, the Bible states that you should never end your day in an argument. He always said that a person should never go to bed angry with anyone. My father said that it is best to apologize to that person by saying that you are sorry.

Q: What factors do you identify as obstacles to your success?
A: Negative feedback—that includes people who do not want to see me succeed and would try to hurt me, when I am trying to advance myself. These negative remarks make me reevaluate myself. I have to tell myself that I will succeed regardless of who is trying to stand in my way.

Q: Do you encounter this negative feedback from peers?
A: Most negative feedback comes from my peers. Sometimes my parents say that my peers are jealous. I am the type of person who tries to give positive feedback to others. If I do not have anything positive to say, I try not to say anything at all. Now that I attend college, I have noticed that all the negative feedback that I am getting is from my black friends.

Q: Do most of your peers attend college?
A: Most of my peers did attend college. A few of my friends are attending college now, and some of them have the same status in college as I do.

Q: What course of action do you take to overcome the obstacles that you have encountered?
A: I continue to be focused. I always think about how I feel about my life and remind myself that I am in control and I am going to reach my goal.

Q: What is your major?
A: My major is biology.

Q: Do you see any obstacles that would keep you from graduate school?
A: I have already been accepted into graduate school, because I was able to keep a high grade point average. The only problem that I had in my major was the math requirement. Math is my weakness, but I learned to get through the rough times by being persistent and dedicated.

Q: What thoughts pass through your mind when making a decision?
A: In regard to selecting a major, the first thought was how happy I would be to work with people in the field of biology for the rest of my life. I also thought about the financial gain. Both reasons were important to me.

Q: What field of biology are you interested in?
A: When I complete graduate school, I am going to become a doctor. As a young child I was always interested in the function of bones, and I was always curious about the way the body works.

Q: What is inside you that motivates you to succeed?
A: The strong will to overcome all obstacles. My strong will proves that negative feedback can be overcome. I know that I am going to succeed. Now, I use negative feedback from others as a positive motivation to achieve my hopes and dreams in life. I know that I am going to succeed, because I am motivated in my heart to do so.

Q: Who are the major influences in your life?
A: The major influences in my life are my parents. My parents have given me a strong spiritual and emotional background.

Q: Did any of your teachers help?
A: Many of the professors helped me by encouraging and motivating me to express myself. My professors have also encouraged me to express myself in written papers—to find my voice—not to keep everything bundled up inside. They would encourage me to "open up," speak up in class.

Q: Were you involved in athletics when you were growing up?
A: I was never really athletically inclined.

Q: Who is your role model?
A: My major role model is my mother, because she is a strong woman, who seems to always have a solution or an answer. I feel that my mother is a very positive force in my life.

Q: When you filled out the biographical profile form, you wrote that your grandmother and grandfather were 100 percent involved in your upbringing. How were they involved?
A: My grandmother and grandfather were basically our babysitters. My mom was really worried about us being exposed to abuse and germs [from] a babysitter. My grandparents took us in, and they molded us, protected us, and they financed my way through college. My grandparents were always there for me.

Q: Is their home close to your home?
A: They live about five minutes away.

Q: Do they keep in touch with you while you are in college?
A: Yes, they do.

Q: Do your mother and father keep in touch with you?
A: Yes, they do. I hear from my parents at least three times a week.

Q: What activities and organizations are important to you?
A: I love volunteer activities, such as cleaning up. This allows me to give back to the community. I also like to be involved in student support services.

Q: Have you experienced any abuse in your life?
A: I have never experienced any abuse in my life. I have always had close friends who told me of their abuse; they opened my eyes to abuse.

Q: Can you think of an abusive relationship that you can relate?

A: One of my friends told me that her father sexually abused her, but when I see their relationship now, it is really hard for me to understand how forgiving she is—seeing their relationship makes me confused.

Q: Have you witnessed any violence in your life?

A: Yes, I have witnessed one of my close neighbors actually being shot by a policeman. As he went to pull out his wallet, he was shot down. My neighbor was not armed; that was my first experience with violence.

Q: Was he injured? Did he die?

A: He was injured. Eventually, he was placed in a mental hospital. People said that he was crazy. He was released from the mental institution, but soon after, he committed suicide.

Q: Did that result from the gun injury?

A: Many people said that all of the hatred and the many years he spent in the mental institution [were] built up inside him. But he had a family and children to live for.

Q: Whom did he hate?

A: I think he probably was against whites and law enforcement officers. He was probably just angry with everyone.

Q: How do you define success?

A: Success is reaching any goal that you set for yourself. It does not matter how small or big that goal is. Once you reach the goal that you set—that is success.

Q: What goals have you reached?

A: I set the goal to graduate from high school, and I achieved that goal. I set the goal to keep my grades at 3.0, and I have. So far, I [have] accomplished my goals. I feel good about myself.

Q: In your opinion, why do you think so many teenage girls become unwed mothers?

A: My friend, who was abused by her father when she was young, is now pregnant by her current boyfriend. I think that she was looking for someone to love and someone to love her. I think that is the major reason for her getting pregnant; she is going to keep the child.

Q: Who is going to take care of the child?

A: I don't know if her boyfriend is going to be there for her, but I know she is going to do everything within her power to raise that child in a single-parent home.

Q: Is her family supportive of her?

A: No, her family is not supportive of her at all. She was on her own since she was sixteen years old.

Q: Where is she living?
A: She is living in the Scott Projects in Miami.

Q: Who is she living with?
A: She is living with her boyfriend.

Q: Do you know of any [other] problems in her family that might be factors for her actions?
A: I have seen drug abuse, alcohol abuse, and violence—all of those factors.

Q: Can you discuss her background?
A: Yes, [her] brothers and cousins were involved in drugs. Her mother was an alcoholic, and her father used cocaine. Her whole family used some type of drug.

Q: Why do you think people get involved in drugs?
A: In the ghetto, people use drugs to escape from their real-life problems. Sometimes, I hear people saying, "I just want to get away tonight and feel high." I think it is really an attempt to escape.

Q: What recommendations do you have for younger black women in the community?
A: My number one recommendation is to get your education. Also, try to have a stable income, and a stable family, before bringing children into the picture.

Q: Why do you think youngsters carry guns to school, [and] oftentimes shoot [them]?
A: I feel that children bring guns to school to frighten others, because they were frightened themselves. I think children are just acting out what has been done to them.

Q: Why is violence more prevalent in this generation?
A: Young children see violence everywhere—television, movies, magazines, newspapers, the neighborhood that they live in; the violent image is constant.

Q: From your perspective, what can be done to control violence?
A: The fear of imprisonment is not going to keep violence suppressed. Guns are too available to the young; banning guns is the only solution.

Q: Do you wish to share any other thoughts for this project?
A: I would like to say that [individuals] can surpass obstacles once they remain fixed on a steady course. Also, they should try to reach their goals by putting the past behind them and looking forward to the future. They should also try to make a better future for themselves and for their children.

Observer's Comments about Respondent

- is good at analysis;

- is dependable;
- has an interest in the arts as well as the sciences.

INTERVIEW 13

Q: What factors do you identify as contributing to your success?
A: My parents always instilled in me that education is very important. They often taught me that without a good education I would not get anywhere. I always think about the confidence they have in me. Because of their encouragement, I decided to attend college.

Q: Did your mother and father bring you up?
A: Yes.

Q: Who was the most influential in your life?
A: I would say my mother, because we had a good relationship; we were always close. My mother and I could talk about everything. My father always worked a lot, but my mother was always there.

Q: Did your mother work?
A: Yes. My mother worked during the day, and my father worked during the night. At night, my mother was home with us.

Q: What type of work does your father do?
A: My father is retired now, but he worked at Ford Motor company from 11:00 p.m. to 8:00 a.m.

Q: What factor do you identify as an obstacle to your success?
A: The factor that I can identify as an obstacle is my shyness. I really do not like to talk in front of a group. That obstacle has really affected me.

Q: Are you becoming less shy now?
A: I am still a little shy, but I am trying.

Q: Can you describe your neighborhood?
A: My neighborhood was a mixture of black and white people.

Q: Did the two groups get along?
A: In some neighborhoods, they did not, but in my neighborhood, they did.

Q: Would you describe your home?
A: I lived in a three-bedroom house with my parents, brother and sister. My sister and I shared a room, up until the time I entered college.

Q: Was there any violence in your neighborhood?
A: There was not any violence in my neighborhood, but a couple blocks down there was always trouble.

Q: Could you tell us about the trouble?
A: Drug-related violence, black on black crime, and gangs.

Q: Can you tell us anything about the gangs in your neighborhood?
A: I really did not know too much about them; my parents kept my sister and I sheltered. I only heard about the violence on the news.

Q: Did you personally know of anyone who became involved selling drugs?
A: I knew someone who was selling drugs. When I went to high school, some of the guys sold drugs, but I didn't know them personally.

Q: Did you have friends in high school?
A: Yes, I did, but not many.

Q: Did your peer group influence you?
A: They didn't influence me, but they influenced my sister. My sister is the opposite of me. She parties and goes out a lot.

Q: Who are the major influences in your life?
A: My mother, father, and godmother are the major influences in my life.

Q: Was your godmother related to you?
A: My godmother was my mother's best friend. When I was born, she became my godmother.

Q: Did any teacher have an influence in your life?
A: In high school, my eleventh grade physiology teacher was a big influence.

Q: Are you involved in the church?
A: When I go back home, I attend church.

Q: Was attending church an important part of your growing up?
A: When I was growing up, we attended church every Sunday. When I go home on vacation, and for the summer, I go to the same church.

Q: How did the church influence you?
A: The church taught me to respect my elders and to be positive. It also taught me to never let my peers influence me to do anything wrong.

Q: What activities were you involved in?
A: I was involved in the youth gospel choir in church and Sunday school.

Q: What organizations were you involved in?
A: I was not involved in any organizations.

Q: Why was church and Sunday school so important?
A: It was important because my mother and grandmother grew up in the church—it was a tradition.

Q: What thoughts pass through your mind when making a decision?
A: Any decision that I make would involve thinking about whether my mother would be proud of me, or not. I would consider in my heart if I was doing the

right thing. Most of all, I would be concerned about my mother supporting my actions. If she would not, I would not become involved.

Q: What is inside you that motivates you to succeed?
A: The fact that I will be the first one in my immediate family to graduate from college. My sister went to college, but she got pregnant and went home. My brother is a freshman in college. My mother went to college, but she never graduated, and my father only graduated from high school. I would definitely be the first person in my immediate family to graduate from college.

Q: In your heart, would graduating from college be a success story?
A: It surely would be a success story for my family and me.

Q: What recommendations would you give to young black women in the community?
A: I would recommend that young black woman always stay positive and put God first in all things. Also, I would recommend that they think about the consequences of their actions before making decisions.

Q: Give me an example of what you think would be a wrong decision, and, then, what you think would be a right decision.
A: I believe that getting involved in drugs is wrong. I believe that staying in school and getting a good education is right.

Q: Do you wish to share any more of your thoughts?
A: I would like to encourage others to stay positive, go to school, and put God first.

Q: What do you mean by putting God first?
A: You should always think about God when making a decision, because he will be the One to judge you. Never do drugs; never let peers influence you into making bad decisions. Think positive.

Observer's Comments about Respondent

- is still shy and quiet;
- recently joined a sorority;
- becoming more expressive in class.

INTERVIEW 14

Q: What factors do you identify as contributing to your success?
A: It was actually basketball that made me take things seriously. It made me maintain a good grade point average, because I knew that I needed good grades to keep playing the game. It also made me a stronger woman and motivated me to achieve my goals.

Q: What or who introduced you to basketball?

A: A friend introduced me to playing basketball. She said that I looked like a basketball player. She also said that I had the talent to play basketball. I tried out for the team, and I made it. Then, a lady, M. B., encouraged me to continue.

Q: Do you consider M. B. your mentor or role model?

A: When I was young, A. L. was always by my side; I would consider her my mentor. But both played significant roles in my life. I really would have to consider M. B. a role model, too, because she made me realize the opportunities that I should take advantage of. She also made me realize that life is serious.

Q: Is your father living in the home?

A: My father is not living in the home.

Q: Would you discuss some of your mother's attributes?

A: My mother is a hardworking, strong parent. She has always taught me how to be a strong woman. I grew up with my mother, and she took care of us [two daughters, one son] by doing the best she could. My mother was always there, encouraging us to make a better future for ourselves than what she made for herself. She instilled in me the importance of having a good education.

Q: Were your mother and father married? Was your father living in the home while you were growing up?

A: My mother and father were not married. My father lived with us until I was seven years old. He then was arrested and went to prison.

Q: What was his crime?

A: I really don't know, but I do know that he was very abusive to my mother. His family is from Georgia, and he committed a crime when he was there. He is suffering the consequences of whatever he did; he has been in jail for a long time now.

Q: Is he in the state prison?

A: Yes, he is in the state prison.

Q: Do you communicate with him?

A: Yes, I do communicate with him, often. He writes us letters, and we communicate with him on the phone. He knows that I am in college playing basketball. My father knows my sister is a correctional officer, and my brother is doing O.K. He really does not have to worry about me, because he knows that I am trying to make a good future for myself.

Q: Does he act more gentle now in his communications?

A: Yes, he does. By the way he talks to my mother and me on the phone, I can tell that he really has changed his life around. He really wants to be a good father now.

Q: Is he the father of all of your mother's children?
A: Yes, he is.

Q: What factors do you identify as obstacles in your life?
A: Thinking negatively is an obstacle. I overcome obstacles by thinking positively. When I was younger, I always had big dreams in life that I am going to make it and achieve my goals. I wanted to become a successful basketball player, and with the help of my mother and my mentor, I kept going. The strong belief that I would never give up made me into the person that I am today. When life gets hard, I concentrate on positive thinking. I always had dreams and goals, and my eyes were fixed on achieving success; so far, it works.

Q: Did you have a vision of yourself living and working outside your neighborhood? What did you daydream about?
A: I was always a home girl, who watched television. Despite everything that was out there, I saw my future as being a movie star on television. Despite the violence and crime out there, I had positive dreams for myself. For example, I wanted to be like Whitney Huston. And I always had the dream to make it to the [W]NBA [Women's National Basketball Association]. But my number one dream is to become a movie star.

Q: What role do you want to play?
A: I want to play the role of a strong, independent woman, who would stand up for what she believes is right—the kind of person who would not let anyone discourage her.

Q: Is that how you see yourself?
A: Yes. I see myself as a strong, independent woman.

Q: Would you describe your home?
A: My home is a nice area in Overtown [inner city]. My home is really safe; there are security guards around the gate, and no one can get in without a key. The landlord doesn't play games; she doesn't allow anyone on the property, unless they live there.

Q: Is there street crime in your neighborhood?
A: Crimes happen every day. Many of my friends, who I grew up with, got shot, and they were like brothers to me. The crime scares me and makes me want to get my mother and whole family out of there. This encourages me to pursue my dreams even more, no matter how hard it gets.

Q: What kind of violence have you seen?
A: I have seen drive-by shootings. Guys come up to other guys with guns, saying that they owe them money. If the guys do not give them money, they will shoot them; that is the kind of crimes that I have seen.

Q: Did they shoot them?
A: Yes, they shot them.

Q: Have you seen them shoot randomly?
A: Yes. I have.

Q: Is it mostly young people who get into trouble in your neighborhood?
A: Mostly young people from the age of nineteen to twenty-six. They are the ones who cause the problems over money to buy drugs. They kill people for drug money.

Q: What kind of drugs?
A: All types of drugs are used on the street.

Q: What is the most commonly used drug?
A: Crack rock is most commonly used.

Q: Is crack rock?
A: Yes, crack is rock.

Q: Are there homeless people in Overtown?
A: Yes. Overtown has the highest population of homeless people. They really do not consider themselves homeless; they are just out there trying to make a living. They have a lot of shelters where they can get something to eat. I think they choose to be homeless.

Q: Do the homeless cause any crimes?
A: No. They do not cause any crimes. Sometimes they buy drugs, but it is the young guys who are out there hungry for drug money. The young guys are out there killing people for a little bit of money, such as twenty-five dollars.

Q: Why do you think these young people take the track that they do?
A: I believe it is the parents' fault, because the parents are not doing what they are supposed to do. The parents are shopping and doing all sorts of things, rather than supporting their kids. The parents should be there encouraging their kids to go to school and [stressing] the importance of a good education. I feel that the parents are not showing their kids enough attention, so the kids go out doing things just for attention. The kids are out there stealing and doing all sorts of crimes. They are killing their own kind.

Q: Is it black-on-black crime?
A: Yes, it is black-on-black crime.

Q: How can a single mother raise her child safely and keep the [child] away from negative situations?
A: My mother has always been a single parent, who has raised us alone, from the time I was seven years old; now, I am twenty years old. It is very hard to be a single parent; you might have to struggle sometimes, but you should always talk to your kids. You should let them know that although there is not a father present in the home, you will be father and mother. Always let them know the importance of a good education and try to be there at home to talk

to them. Set good moral standards for the children to follow. Do not neglect your kids; they will understand that although they do not have a father in the home, they do have a loving mother who cares. There are many strong, independent women, who are out there doing a good job.

Q: Do you have girlfriends that got pregnant early in life?
A: Yes. I have one best friend who got pregnant. I feel that the reason she got pregnant was because her parents stopped showing her attention when she became eighteen. When her parents stopped showing her attention, she began to live the fast life and became a stripper. She dropped out of school when she was in the tenth grade, but I continued in school. We still keep in contact with each other. Recently, she turned her life around for the better and stopped stripping. [Unfortunately,] she is twenty years old and pregnant with her third kid, but she has a strong man that is there for them.

Q: What are her feelings about her choices in life?
A: She said she wished that she was not on her third kid. She also wished that she would have finished school and got a good job. I guess her parents were not there for her to encourage her to continue in school. But parents can only do so much; if she wanted to finish school, she had the opportunity. She could have completed her education, but she preferred the other way.

Q: After having one child out of wedlock, why would she get pregnant the second and third time?
A: Actually, I talk to her all the time and ask her why she would make the same mistakes, but she said she does not want to make the same mistakes. I encourage her to use protection, because she has to protect herself against harm and pregnancy. She said she learned from her mistakes, and she is not out there having sex anymore, neither she is stripping.

Q: Would you say she was a prostitute?
A: I do not think she was a prostitute. She was a stripper and followed the other girls.

Q: Is she back at home with her mother and father?
A: She is not back home; she lives with her boyfriend.

Q: Is he the father of all three of the kids?
A: Yes, most definitely.

Q: What are the major influences in your life?
A: The major influence in my life is family; they always stood by my side. My family made me continue with my education; they were always so proud of me.

Q: Is athletic involvement influential?
A: If it was not for sports, I would not be here today. Basketball is the reason why I came to Florida Memorial College. Without my interest in basketball,

I do not know where I would be today; my interest in sports helps me to fulfill my hopes and dreams.

Q: Does the church play a role?
A: Yes, the people that I meet in church also give me encouragement to seek out after my dreams.

Q: Do you believe that community organizations are important in helping the young to find a way?
A: Yes. I would encourage children to become a part of any positive organization that would educate them to live the right lifestyle and think positive.

Q: What thoughts pass through your mind when making a decision?
A: I would think about the importance of college; I would not make a decision detrimental to my getting a college degree. I don't make decisions that would prevent me from studying hard and establishing good time management skills. I know college is serious, and most of all, I know I have to make the grade to play basketball.

Q: What is your major?
A: My major is physical education.

Q: How do you define success?
A: I would define success as reaching your hopes and dreams in life; part of success is having the motivation to strive daily to reach the goals you set; success will come if you never give up.

Q: What advice would you give to other black women in the community?
A: I would encourage them to overcome their problems in life by working hard and finding a way. Do not let anybody discourage you from achieving your goals. You should always have a strong and positive attitude about your future.

Q: What would you like to say to children growing up in the inner city?
A: I would like to encourage them to go after their dreams.

Observer's Comments about Respondent

- is very tall and physically strong;
- is a star player for the college basketball team;
- feels fortunate to have a mentor and role model in her life;
- is a good listener.

INTERVIEW 16

Q: What factors do you identify as contributing to your success?
A: I would say high school teachers who became my mentors.

Q: Can you give an example of what a teacher might have contributed?

A: My freshman English teacher showed me how to improve my writing so that I would have a chance in college. She showed interest in my work from my freshman year of high school until I graduated. She was my teacher for three years. In my freshman year, I got a D in her class; in my junior year, I got an A. She showed me different ways to improve my writing—what to look for, what to expect when I got to college.

Q: What person or persons in your family contributed to your success?

A: Mostly, my mom. But my dad, too. But mostly my mom. She didn't have the chance to go to college when she was younger—no one in her family had the money. I don't think she ever tried to get a loan to go to college. She wanted me to have the chance to go to college. I am grateful that my father wanted me to go to college, too. He told me that college is the right way to go. He said that if I didn't go right after [high school], then I probably would never go. He told me that college was for people that wanted to make something of themselves.

Q: On your biographical sheet, you wrote that your mother brought you up without your dad being at home. Was that difficult for her?

A: It was very difficult. I stayed with my mom all my life; she was a single parent. My dad was there from time to time, but it was pretty hard coming up because I didn't have a father figure in the house to tell me what to do and how to do it. He always lived somewhere else. My mom always told us that she never had the chance to do very much with her life and that we should grow up and be successful. My dad, on the other hand, tried so hard to talk to us, but because he was not with us, it was very hard to understand his advice. It was a very difficult situation trying to grow up in a house, seeing my mom struggling, and trying—being the oldest—to understand everything. I learned a lot of things faster than some other kids—I had to learn little, but important, things. When I was five and six years old, I had to learn how to climb a fire escape, to cook for my little sister (a year younger than me), because mommy, of course, had to work and make the money. Now that I am older, it is a little easier, because I get to see different things and see how to do it the right way, so I won't have the same problems as my mom. I am not knocking her for it, but I just want to try harder and wait to get married to have kids. My mom, on the other hand, didn't wait, she had kids before she got married; but I don't have any regrets, and I don't think she does either. She just moves on each day, and so do I.

Q: How many children does your mother have?

A: My mom has two kids: my sister and I. My sister is a year younger than me; my dad has five children. On both sides, I am the oldest.

Q: Is your dad the father of your sister as well?

A: Yes, he is.

Q: Do you know why your mom and dad didn't get married?
A: I think my mom was very young-minded; my dad was in college when my mom got pregnant, so he couldn't continue in college. They had a lot of differences that they could never work out, and I really don't know why their relationship didn't work, but I know that my dad is a very hard man to deal with, and my mom is too fuzzy, so each one contributed to the problems.

Q: Does your father live in the same city as you do?
A: Yes, he does. He lives about fifteen minutes away. When I was younger—from ten years old downward—I hardly saw my dad. If I went to my grandmother's house, I saw him. My dad never associated with my mom for a long time. He was behind in paying benefits for his kids. My mom and dad had two kids together; he needed to see his children when they were young, but he only wanted to be a part of his children's life when they got older.

Q: What does he do for a living?
A: My dad is a state trooper for the state of Connecticut.

Q: What kind of work does your mother do?
A: My mom works as a dispatch operator for a corporation.

Q: What factors do you identify as obstacles to your success?
A: When I was younger, the number one factor would be my dislike of reading.

Q: What helps you to overcome obstacles?
A: Listening to friends who are excelling in college. They have helped me to think about my future. Each day, I take a little step forward to improve myself. Now, I constantly think about improvement. I now enjoy reading, and I understand the importance of learning from reading good books.

Q: What subjects do you study?
A: I am trying to improve my knowledge every day; I try to improve my handwriting every day; I try to improve my reading every day; I try to improve my vocabulary every day; I try to improve my motivation, and each day I take a step toward reaching my goal—a theater career. I also try to improve the way I look at life—from past to present. I try to do things a little bit differently every day, a little bit better every day.

Q: Are you hard on yourself?
A: I am very lenient at times; I am very lenient because I don't want to work myself too hard, because I get tired. But when I set my mind to doing something I am hard on myself, and, yes, sometimes I work on something, regardless of how I feel. My dad is very hard on me; he doesn't play any games when it comes to school. If he knew I was as lenient as I am on myself, he wouldn't like it. Going to college made me grow up. I got to learn things for myself; I have no one to depend on, only myself.

Q: Were your peers influential in your life?
A: Yes. They influenced me to go to college, because I would always hear them talking about college. I never wanted to go to college right after graduating from high school. I wanted to wait a couple of years, but I decided to go because my peers went.

Q: What was the worst experience in your life?
A: The worst experience in my life was my freshman year in college; I played around; I was not serious; I didn't do any assignments; my freshman year was terrible. I was somewhere else. I became very stressed out, and I started to have anxiety attacks. I wasn't in the right state of mind; it was a nightmare. At the time, I wanted to be in the "in crowd." I eventually learned that I needed to concentrate on my assignments. I realized that my friends can't get me my grades, and I would have to take responsibility for myself. That's when I started to do better.

Q: Were there any negative pressures by your peers?
A: Yes. My high school friends were negative on my dreams to become involved in the performing arts. They often said that I wouldn't make it in theater or television—that the competition was too fierce. But, I did a commercial for a theme park in Connecticut, and I might do another one this summer. In looking back, I feel I did accomplish my goal, and they shouldn't have knocked my dreams.

Q: Have you been involved in athletics?
A: Yes, in high school, I played basketball and ran track. I don't know how I managed to keep up my grades, but I did. In the beginning of my junior year, I hurt my knee running; it was then that I started to get interested in the performing arts—dance and drama. I was dancing for about seven years before I even went into the performing arts.

Q: Are you involved in the church?
A: Yes. I am a Christian. I always try to attend church every Sunday, not because I was made to go, but because I choose to go. I think a person has to put the Lord first in his or her life before they can become successful.

Q: Have you seen any violence in your neighborhood?
A: Oh yes! I used to live in the inner city of Hartford [Connecticut,] and I have seen everything. I used to live close to a club, and I remember one day waking up because it was so noisy. I opened the window, and I saw people acting crazy and shooting at each other. It was bad. I've seen people stabbing one another. I've seen people on the ground in pools of their own blood. I've seen a lot of violence, but that was something to stay away from. The best thing that I can do is pray and hope that these people try to get their life together. I feel I got my life together. I am in college, and when I go home, I

now live in the outskirts, and I don't come in contact with those kind of people.

Q: What was the cause of the violence?
A: The first reason for the violence is drugs. The second reason is fights because of jealousy. When a man and woman go to a club as a couple, the woman may end up dancing with someone else. Her date will get upset and go after the man that she is dancing with. These fights start from jealousy; much of the violence stems from jealousy.

Q: Do you think drugs are the source of most of the crimes?
A: Yes. Drugs are a big part of the problem. I think drive-by shootings are caused by drug wars. Even little kids get involved. Most fights are caused by drugs. When I was living across the street from the club, somebody knocked on my door looking for the last tenant, who sold drugs. I was so scared, but I couldn't do anything. All I could do was pray that the Lord would help me; I wasn't really strong into the church at that time, but I had to say, "Lord help me."

Q: Has your father confirmed that a lot of the drive-by shootings, and violence in general, [are] caused by drugs?
A: I think so, I think so. I've been in the car with my dad while he was on a chase. He is a state trooper. In and out of uniform, he could pull over and help people. He happened to be without his uniform, and he was pulling a car over, while I was in the car. Suddenly, the person ran; all I can remember is my dad getting out and running, jumping over a fence, and before I knew it, he was out of sight. The only thing I could think of was that the person had drugs. Why else would he run? I think my dad can confirm that.

Q: Which drugs are the most prevalent?
A: I would say marijuana and cocaine. Maybe some heroin, but I am not sure. Most of the drug dealing involves a lot of money.

Q: What thoughts pass through your mind when making a decision?
A: What type of decision?

Q: A decision that is a life strategy decision, for instance going to college?
A: The thoughts that pass through my mind [are]: how can this benefit me? What am I getting out of it? What part do I play? What do I have to do? Will I be successful? Is this something that I want to do? Even though I can answer "Yes" to these questions, I still consider [them] further.

Q: Does your mother or your father come to mind when making a decision?
A: For the most part, I would say my mom, because I try to do things that she never had the chance to do, or didn't have the money to do, or didn't have the courage to do. She wants me to go much further in my life than she did in her life. But when it comes to financial support, I would say my dad, because he

pays for my college. He has the money, so I go to my dad for money, but, other than that, I go to my mom first.

Q: Can you describe the home that you grew up in?
A: I moved about. During grammar school and high school, I moved probably seven to eight times. In and out, in and out. The majority of times, up until my high school years, I was in the inner city, so I experienced violence, all kinds of pollution, all kinds of crazy people, all kinds of things—a crazy place to live.

Q: Did any of your grandparents play a part in your going to college?
A: Yes, I would say both my mother's side and my father's side. My mother's side never had the chance to go to college, but they encouraged me. On both sides, they always told me that I was the oldest grandchild, and they encouraged me. It was the first time that I realized that my father's parents cared about me. My mother's father died two years ago, so he didn't really have the chance to see me go to college, but I am sure he knew that I was going.

Q: How do you define success?
A: Success is making a decision and going for it. Success is something that I had to think about. I had to make a decision about a goal, and then work toward it. Success is working and motivating yourself. Success is being strong, and most important, being ready for improvement—so you will be successful.

Q: What do you mean by being ready?
A: If you want to do something, you have to plan it out. Like me, I knew I wanted theater, so I went toward that goal: got the newspaper, found out where the performing arts schools were, got an application, auditioned, got accepted, and continued to work toward that goal. I started to take the first steps in high school–I knew what I wanted and went for it. Now, I am halfway there.

Q: Previously, you mentioned not being serious; now, you seem very serious. What was the turning point in your thoughts?
A: I thought about my mom not picking up on her own, wasting a lot of time. She was the type of person that waited for the last minute to do everything, and she really didn't strive as hard as she should have. My dad has always been very direct; he knew what he wanted; he went for it. My dad tries everything. If it wasn't for my dad pushing me, I would be a person that wasted time, too. My mom is my mom; my dad is my dad; I have to be me.

Q: If you had to choose your mom or dad as a role model, who would you choose?
A: That's a hard decision. For the most part, I would have to say definitely dad, definitely dad. He gives us [his children] whatever he didn't have when he was younger; he goes that extra mile for us. My mom does, too; my mom

is good to talk to. She and I are very tight. But my dad is a good role model for success; he put me in the place that I am in right now.

Q: What are the positive traits that he has?
A: He went to college. My father went to a junior college, and he went to West Virginia State. My dad has two degrees; one in recreation and one in law. My dad is married, has a big house, and [has] large investments. He owns a little bit of property.

Q: How old is your mom?
A: My mom is forty, and my dad is forty-one.

Q: And how old was she when she got pregnant with you?
A: My mom was twenty-two, and my dad was twenty-three.

Q: Were they neighborhood friends?
A: No. My dad was in college, and my mom was in cosmetology school. They were in West Virginia. I lived there for a couple of years.

Q: What activities and organizations can you identify as helping you in your development?
A: I was in the NAACP [National Association for the Advancement of Colored People]. It was important to me; the counselors help young people go in the right direction. I have been a member for the last five or six years. I used to be a secretary for a youth organization in Connecticut, an organization that helps young people find summer jobs. I've been working with them for about four or five years, and I have the same job. This summer, they are going to give me an internship, which pays thirteen dollars an hour. They want to create a positive environment for the young in the city of Hartford.

Q: Who do you look like, your mom or your dad?
A: I look like my dad and have traits of my mom, but I have both of them in me.

Q: Who has a light complexion in your family?
A: My mom is really light. My dad is light, but my mom is lighter. My mom is really light; I have her complexion, but my dad's face. I really look like my dad. If he [put] on weight, we would look just alike. That's how much we look alike.

Q: Have you ever been prejudiced against?
A: When I was younger, I was prejudiced against: I didn't know the meaning of segregation. Everybody deserves a chance. Color really doesn't matter a lot to me; I realize that some people think I am white; yet some people think I am black; some people think I am mixed. I get different viewpoints from different people, and I listen. But I am not affected; to me, it's interesting to meet different kinds of people. In that way, I get to have different experi-

ences–with food, places, interactions. My mom taught me right, and I am not prejudiced at all.

Q: What is your mother's background?
A: My mother's background, as far as I know, is black, but I think way back, her family line was really light. My dad is black for the most part, as far as I can learn from my family tree.

Q: Do you have a preference in dating light-skinned or dark-skinned men?
A: I used to have a preference for light-skinned people. I don't know why. Maybe because I am light skinned, but now, it doesn't really matter to me. I like to date different people and understand different races, and right now, I am talking to a person who is Haitian. That's really different for me.

Q: What recommendations do you have for younger black women?
A: I would say, strive for your dreams. Don't stop striving. Never let anyone knock you down. Have faith in yourself. If you try something and it doesn't work, and you fall, get back up, try again. Be willing to try something else. Don't be afraid. Put your full effort into your decisions. Trust yourself.

Observer's Comments about Respondent

- did an about face;
- changed from lack of seriousness to being very serious;
- changed from immaturity to maturity.

INTERVIEW 20

Q: What factors do you identify as contributing to your success?
A: I would have to say my mom, because when I decided to go back to school, she was the first person that I spoke to. I had an idea, and I needed her feedback. I didn't want to be a nurse anymore. I really wanted to teach. I told her that I was quitting my job, so that I could go back to school and get a degree in education. I asked her if she could help by taking care of the kids. My mom has been so supportive. She is giving of herself, more than 200 percent. She keeps my daughters. Days that I am just exhausted, and although my mom also works her own job, she will work, she'll wash, she'll cook, she'll clean. Without her, I wouldn't have been able to do it. If I didn't have the emotional support from my mom, I would not even go back to school. [And] with the help of the Lord—without him it would not have been possible for me to get from point A to B.

Q: Does your religious faith play an important part in your life?
A: I have a strong faith. When I graduated from high school in 1992, I already had my daughters. I went to college, but it wasn't right. I was young, had two

kids, didn't know what to do with my life. I always wanted better for myself, but I just didn't know a path. I just didn't know how to walk a path. I just had no direction, and it took me at least five years—then I became Christian. When I became Christian and put my trust in [the Lord], it just seemed like doors started to open. It hasn't been easy, but I have direction now. I did not have direction before. I was so young and so immature, trying to raise babies and I was still the baby. I didn't know what to do; I didn't know where to go, but now I am focused. I finally know where I want to be and where I want to go.

Q: Did you have two babies when you were in high school?
A: Yes, I had two kids when I was in high school.

Q: Were you a teenage unwed mom?
A: Yes, I was a teenage [unwed] parent. I had [one child] when I was fifteen, and I had [a second child] when I was seventeen.

Q: Did you want to get pregnant?
A: When you associate girls with having babies, you associate the hot mamas. The ones that are fast in the behind. I wasn't like that. My boyfriend was just somebody that I met. I didn't know anything about boys; my mom and I didn't talk about sex. We didn't discuss anything like that. But I remember the one time I asked her about sex, she said, "It didn't even feel good; don't do it," and she made a scene like it must not be good. But, she was doing it! We didn't discuss it after that scene.

Q: Can you discuss your relationship with the man who fathered your children?
A: He was somebody I met; he was older than me, I didn't know anything about boys or sex. I didn't date. My mom didn't let me talk on the phone with boys. When I had sex the first time, I got pregnant. It just happened. I got pregnant. I didn't want to have a baby. Something just happened and happened twice.

Q: Do the two children have the same father?
A: Yes, they have the same father.

Q: Did you ever think about getting married?
A: Not with him, but I will eventually get married—but not with him.

Q: Why not?
A: Well, because he never took care of [his children. One] is almost ten and [the second child] is eleven. He never changed, never changed. He is immature. He hasn't taken responsibility; he's still the immature person that I met. He hasn't grown up over the years. I think my children have more sense than he has.

Q: What is the cause of the problems that seem to haunt African American men?
A: I have dated black men; not all black men are bad. There are some really good, strong brothers who take on their responsibilities, who have jobs and

are good providers. College is not for everyone, but I think some of our black males are influenced by the wrong things. They listen to rap; it influences them. They become money hungry. Money and women, money and women, that's all they want, and they think that is all they need. They get money, and they get laid. They have no direction; they are not focused. But [that] might not be a fair assessment. I see the brothers in my neighborhood that walk the streets all night, trying to sell drugs on the corner. However, I also see the young men who go to class, motivated to become doctors, lawyers, or teachers. So, I would have to say that sometimes perceptions are limited to where you grow up. If you grow up in a ghetto, or similar circumstances, and only see black men who point guns, beat women, sling rocks, skip school, and your daddy is not different, then that's your perception of the African American male. When you go outside that area, you realize that every black man is not like that and perceptions change.

Q: What is the cause of young people straying away from ethical conduct?
A: It is a combination of causes. In my case, my mom didn't teach me that I had choices. She didn't teach me that I could go to college and have a professional career. She didn't tell me that I had a choice to stay a virgin, or that I should wait to choose a husband and not fall into the situation that I did. When you don't know that you have choices, or you're not talked to about certain issues, you're just groping in the wrong places for answers. For example, I learned about sex from my friends, not from my mom. My friends shaped my reality. If I had received the information from my mom and learned that the act of sex should be sacred, I would not have had sex at a young age. Many of the young girls are looking for someone to love them, or for them to love.

Q. How do you overcome obstacles?
A: Strong determination. I have two kids, and I always knew I wanted to achieve, so I had self-determination. I encountered so many obstacles, and I worked through the problems with strong determination. It seems we, as a people, blame others. I see other women who don't have kids; they go to college, get their degrees, and get married. Then they have their kids. And I say to myself, "I wish I would have done it that way." But I can't blame anyone but myself. If I blamed someone else, other than myself, I would be stuck in a rut: "Oh, I'm blaming it on the white man; I'm blaming it on my baby's daddy; I'm blaming it on my momma for not teaching me nothing, I'm blaming. . . ." I think if you keep blaming it on everybody else, then you'll get stuck; you can't move on. I think you just have to accept the consequences of acts, and just move on from there. But a lot of the times, we don't move on. We just spend our lives blaming other people, instead of looking into ourselves and trying to do better.

Q: Is your mother a single parent?
A: Is my mom a single parent? Yeah, she's a single parent.

Q: Was she an unwed mother?

A: I'm an only child, and my mom was single when she got pregnant with me. My dad was already married.

Q: How old was she?

A: Twenty-six; she wasn't young.

Q: Did she ever discuss the circumstances with you?

A: When she met him, she didn't know that he was married. When she found out that she was pregnant, she told my grandmother that she was not ever going to have any more kids, because she could only take care of one child, and that's all she was going to have, and that's all she had—one child, me.

Q: Was your grandmother married?

A: My grandmother has four kids, the first two out of wedlock. She had my mom and my uncle when she was not married. My grandmother was fifteen years old when she had my mom—the same age as me when I had my first child—and she had my uncle when she was seventeen years old, the same age as me when I had my second child. She got married when she was eighteen, already having had two kids. She married my granddad, who is my step-granddad, and then she had two more kids. They are still married.

Q: When you got pregnant at fifteen years old, what was the reaction of your mother and grandmother?

A: They were so hard on me, and they are still hard on me, especially my grandmother. I was the family's last hope. It was like "[She's] so smart, she's going to college, she's gonna do this, she's gonna do that. . . ." I disappointed my grandmother, and I think she still hasn't gotten over it. My mom, I disappointed her, too. I don't know, I think I made up for it, a little bit. One day she came to me and she said, "You know you are a wonderful mother," and I almost dropped to the floor, 'cause my mom never said that before, and I didn't expect it. But I think that they are still disappointed, very disappointed, especially my grandmother. She probably won't be satisfied until she has my degree hanging over her bed, then she'll probably feel better.

Q: You have always impressed me as being sensible.

A: Really, well, that's funny. I didn't always have good sense.

Q: What or who were the major influences in your life?

A: I'm a Christian, and it was only by the grace of God. But also my mom, of course, and two members of my church, S. and L., have been the most influential. Ms. S. is like my aunt; we are really like family now. She has been one person who doesn't care how bad her day has been; her house could have burnt down, her kids gone, husband gone, and I can call her with a problem, less than hers, and she will take the time to encourage me. I don't care what time of night it is, or if she is in the middle of a shower. I could just say, "I need to talk," and she would say, "Hold on for a minute, so I can turn the shower off."

Q: What does she say? What does she do?
A: She just pushes me to the point that I can't walk, anymore; I can't do it, anymore. And, she says, "Yes you can, yes you can, you can do it." Sister L., too, she's like my grandmother. They just keep me geared up. When I say, "I'm tired of going to school, the kids aren't acting right, I wanna be married, I wanna be this, that . . . my life is an ordeal, and my faith is gone."

Q: How do you feel after you listen to them?
A: It's like a sugar rush. When I need something sweet, those are the people I call, and I need something sweet all the time, so I call them every day. And my professors, too. I've had some wonderful professors, that not only touched my heart, but have given me that extra push. At times, I questioned the material that I had to learn, and I [said] to myself, "I'm not going to use this; what's the point?" But, the professors are great! I eventually realized that I learned so much from them. Now, I just say to myself: "Oh, I'm going to use this in the classroom. Oh, I'm going to teach this to my students. I'm going to be like Professor B.; I'm going to be like Dr. J."

Q: Have your children been helpful?
A: Yes, my children have been more than helpful. They influenced me, too. They have become more independent. A good example would be in the morning when I am sleeping. They'll come in and give me a kiss and say, "Okay momma we're leaving," and I'll say, "Wait a minute, what time is it?" "It's seven-fifteen, momma, we got to go." They'll be dressed; they ironed their clothes; they fixed their breakfast; they packed their backpacks; they have everything ready to begin the day. They say, "Here momma, here's your keys." They lock the door, and they are gone. On the weekends, they come in and say, "Momma, wake up! We fixed breakfast!" Their cooking has gotten better; they fix grits and eggs. In so many ways, they help me; I haven't cleaned in a year. They switch their chores each week: either they have kitchen or bathroom duty. They gained the independence that I needed from them, and they came through. I needed them to become more independent, while I take on this load, and they did. So, yeah, they have influenced me.

Q: Did you join any activities when you were in high school?
A: Yes, I was in the high school chorus, and FEA and FBLA

Q: What do those acronyms stand for?
A: Future Educators of America, Future Business Leaders of America. I was pretty popular, before and even after I got pregnant. I graduated on time; I went to school until my last day of pregnancy. I was at school when I went into labor. Yeah, I was pretty involved. I think back on it now and say, "God, I wish I was the student then that I am now; I could have done a lot more."

But, then again, I might not have. I can't say, "If I didn't have kids, I would have really been somebody." I might have turned out worse.

Q: What thoughts pass through your mind when making a decision?
A: [Whom] is it going to affect, how is going to impact me, my children, my mom—is it worth it? What are the end results?

Q: Can you describe the home you grew up in?
A: Well, I grew up in a single-parent home, just me and my mom, and my mom has always been a good mother, the best that she knew how to be. There are certain things that my mom did that I found myself doing. Not because we discussed it, but because I watched her, so she became an example. Mom is cool; we were very close; some people say she spoiled me, but I was her only child. My mom has always been an adult. One day I went into her room, and asked her, "How do you like this?" I wanted her impression of what I was wearing. She said, "Well, that looks nice." I said, "What about my hair and makeup?" She answered, "It looks nice, but you are beautiful, you don't have to worry about makeup." And I said, "Well, I look just like you." She said, "Um, I thought I was always so ugly." And my momma and I look just alike. So, I said, "I'm not ugly, you know, I'm not ugly, and we look just alike."

Q: Do you think your mom felt ugly?
A: My mom always had a conflict about herself, and that's how she treated me. Sometimes she was very nasty, and she would call me names. I don't think she really meant to hurt me, because she was hurting herself. I don't know what my grandma did to her. But she never made me feel pretty. She never expressed her feelings with hugs and kisses. Until this day, she and I don't hug and kiss. Like with my grandmother, we never, never hugged when we were little, never. Momma would say, "Oh my God, you better never kiss her, never." Oh my god , if you were to go to her and put your arm around her, she would push you away. It wasn't an affectionate family. Sometimes when my children hug me, it feels so funny. Sometimes they kiss me from the time I walk in the door to the time I go to bed. Kiss, kiss, hug. Sometimes, I'm like "Get away from me, stop it, I'm sick of it." I hurt their feelings, but I wasn't used to that growing up. But my mom dated a lot of men, and she always let them stay with us, and I couldn't understand it. She didn't need them, but I guess she was looking for someone to love her and make her feel beautiful.

Q: How did her actions affect you?
A: Before I became a Christian, when I was younger, I used to have my boyfriend spend the night at my house, and he was like the father of my kids. And I thought back [that] this is what my mother used to do, and I didn't want to do that any more. I didn't want to expose my kids to that kind of behavior, because, I remember, when I was little, men were in my house, in my mother's room with her, and I'm in there, too. I'm saying, "I don't want my kids to grow up with memories like that, so I changed that part of my life." But my

mom raised me the best that she could. She didn't set goals, because she didn't have any set for herself. She didn't push, push, push me about school; she always made me be independent. She didn't ask me about homework. She didn't ask me about report cards. She knew, "Ok, [she] got it; she'll do it by herself."

Q: What kind of work did she do while you were growing up?
A: My momma did housework. Then she went into nursing, and that's what she does now, but she did housework for a long, long time. She used to work for two rich white ladies on Miami Beach. I'll never forget it. Ms. S. and Ms. W., sisters, who lived side by side. They had the biggest, biggest mansion at that time. When school was out, we used to go over there and work. My momma used to take me over there, and they used to let me play with their clothes. I never saw fur coats before. They used to let me get in the pool; they had a yacht, too. They lived in Miami Beach, close to the ocean. They also had fur coats and what seemed like millions of shoes. I think that's where I get my shoe fetish from. I love shoes. I used to be like, "Why is my momma over here cleaning these white people's house; why is she over here, why?" I would never do that, never. And one day, I remember the lady asked me, "When you get older, are you going to come and work for me like your mommy does?" And I told her, "No! I am not going to work for you. I am going to be somebody; I am going to be a lawyer; I am not coming here to work for you." And I remembered the look of my mom's face like, "Tell her baby, you tell her baby, that you are not coming here to work." But, then, she went to nursing school, 1989, something like that, and she has been doing that ever since.

Q: Did she get a four-year degree?
A: No, she got a certificate. She is a LPN [Licensed Practical Nurse]. She wants to go back to school in nursing; she has a couple of more classes to take, but she should go. Maybe, after I finish school, I will encourage her to go back and finish that last year so she can be a nurse.

Q: How old is she now?
A: My mom is fifty-three.

Q: What recommendations would you give to young black women in the community?
A: Don't have any kids. I am so glad my cousin doesn't have any kids. Don't get pregnant, because you can't rectify that. It is not like a bad hair day that you can fix. That baby is always going to be there. From the time [babies] are born, it alters your life; they map out your whole life. Be positive. Do not rely on a man for anything but fertilization. Be independent. First, learn about yourself. I learned so much about myself, what I like; I didn't even have a clue about who I was; now I know who I am. Get to know yourself by being by yourself for a while—go to college. Work; get some independence. Edu-

cate yourself in something, whether you get a certificate for vocational training or you go to medical school. Better yourself, so you can get a better mate. If you aren't nothing, you don't get nothing. If you don't want nothing, you're going to get someone who doesn't want nothing. And you will have nothing, and the kids will have nothing. It's going to be awful. Just be positive, interchange your values [with individuals you admire], really look at what is important and not hang out on South Beach or become obsessed with the latest fashion. But, get to know yourself and be positive about your life. Have a plan, have some focus and direction.

Q: Have you ever experienced violence in your environment?
A: Yes, when I was little, my mom used to date a guy that was very abusive to her, and I used to watch it all the time. I'm talking about very abusive, beating her down, and I used to think: "She doesn't need him. This *red* guy." I think that's why I don't like *red* men—high-yellow, you know, curly hair, blue-green eyes. He looked like the devil, and I used to watch him. They would make up. But she didn't even need him; he didn't work; he didn't contribute anything. My mom always has been independent, even to this day. If my car breaks down, my mom will get out there, before I call a mechanic. She says, "No, no, honey, let me go out there first." If my mom needed her whole house painted, she would go out there and paint it herself. She wouldn't wait for anybody. And I couldn't understand what she needed him for, and I said to myself, "I am never going to let a man hit me!" If he hits me, one of us is going to die that night. When I was younger, I tried to kill a guy for hitting me. I remember that, my lip busted, and all for what? A man to just be around? Well, no woman needs a man to just be around.

Q: What is inside you that motivates you to keep going?
A: That's an easy question. It is only the spirit of the Lord that's inside me that keeps me going. Because sometimes, I don't even want to get up in the morning; I don't want to go to work; I don't even want to deal with my kids. It seems every time you wash the clothes, they pile right back up, my daughters change clothes fifty times a day. Socks missing, and the food runs out, as fast as I buy it. [One] needs a new pair of shoes every week, 'cause her feet keep growing; her feet are bigger than mine. She needs shorts; she is growing out of everything. I just don't know how I make it, sometimes. It is because I say to myself, "It is almost over; I am almost a college graduate—a couple more semesters, and it will be over." Then, I say, "Thank God, I'll have a job, with benefits and good pay, so that I can take care of my kids." Even if I decide not to get a master's or Ph.D. degree, I would be content with what I accomplished. I could put my children through college, and I don't have to worry about going to the welfare place to apply for this and apply for that. I would have finally jumped that hurdle. So that is one of the reasons that keeps me going. I can see the top of the mountain, and I am almost there. These classes try to knock me down, and, sometimes, I just feel like I can't

crawl anymore. But that's when I ask God for strength for another day, so I can get there. That's, basically, the main reason. I know that I have my family counting on me, and I just want to show them that I did it— that I finally did it!

Q: What kind of work are you doing now?
A: I work with the school board. I work at an elementary school.

Q: What is your title?
A: Peer professional 2.

Q: Have you ever depended on government assistance?
A: Yes, when I was younger. It really does help. Everything is so expensive, especially raising kids. I'm not having any more kids until I get married and my husband has a good job.

Q: Do you think that the welfare system is a factor that keeps men from supporting their family and living in the home?
A: No, it does not. If a man wants to take care of his children, he will. My children's father didn't even want to pay $25.00 every two weeks. How low can you get! Some men are so immature. They don't understand. They are vindictive. They forget all about the children. I think welfare could be designed better, but there is nothing wrong with needing assistance. When it first came out, it was for middle class women, who needed help—white women. It's not something bad, but a lot of women abuse the system. Some have good jobs, drive good cars, and still take the money. But a lot of people really need it. When I was younger, I participated in a program that would help people find a job; the job paid $5.20 an hour. I remember they sent me to a warehouse that was full of meat. What was I supposed to do there? They just brushed me off. It's not true that any job is better than none. But some women just say, "Forget it; I'm going to stay on the job and collect the money." I don't think the welfare system keeps men away. Many men are on welfare themselves. They abuse it; they don't take care of their children, but they take care of their girlfriends. Then, they say, "the woman [mother of his children] is getting AFDC [Aid to Families with Dependent Children], so she doesn't need my money." [A man like that] doesn't take care of his own children. How can any father not take care of his own children?

Observer's Comments about Respondent

- is responsible and dedicated;
- has been interning at a high school;
- is excited about her career in teaching;
- will be a role model to her students;
- is one of the best students of English that I ever taught.

References

Addison, R. B. (1992). "Grounded Hermeneutic Research." In B. Crabtree and W. L. Miller (eds.), *Doing Qualitative Research*. Newbury Park, CA: Sage.

Alford, N. M. (1997). *African-American Women's Self-Esteem as a Function of Skin Color: A Quasi-Qualitative Study*. Ann Arbor, MI: UMI Dissertation Services.

Allan, T. J. (1999). "Introduction: Decoding Womanist Grammar of Difference in Womanist and Feminist Aesthetics: A Comparative Review." In H. A. Ervin (ed.), *African American Literary Criticism 1773–2000*, 433–44. New York: Twayne.

Apfel, N. H., & Seitz, V. (1991). "Four Models of Adolescent Mother-Grandmother Relationships in Black Inner-City Families." *Family Relations* 40: 421–29.

Beaulieu, E. A. (1999). *Black Women Writers and the American Neo-Slave Narrative: Femininity Unfettered*. Westport, CT: Greenwood Press.

Belknap, J. (1996). *The Invisible Woman: Gender, Crime, and Justice*. Belmont, CA: Wadsworth.

Bell-Scott, P. (1984, Spring). "Black Women's Higher Education: Our Legacy." *Sage: A Scholarly Journal on Black Women* 1:8–11.

———. (1994). *Life Notes: Personal Writings by Contemporary Black Women*. New York: W. W. Norton.

Bell-Scott, P., & Guy-Sheftall, B. (eds.) (1991). *Double Stitch: Black Women Write about Mothers and Daughters*. Boston: Beacon.

Billingsley, A. (1992). *Climbing Jacob's Ladder: The Enduring Legacy of African American Families*. New York: Simon and Schuster.

Blassingame, J. (1979). *The Slave Community: Plantation Life in the Antebellum South*. New York: Oxford University Press.

Bogdan, R., & Bilken, S. (1982). *Qualitative Research for Education: An Introduction to Theory and Methods*. Boston: Allyn and Bacon.

Bowie, A. (ed.). (1998). *Schleiermacher: Hermeneutics and Criticism and Other Writings*. New York: Cambridge University Press.

Braxton, J. M. (1999). "Ancestral Presence: The Outraged Mother Figure in Contemporary Afra-American Writing." In E. A. Beaulieu (ed.). *Black Woman Writers and the American Neo-Slave Narrative: Femininity Unfettered*. Westport, CT: Greenwood Press.

Brent, L. (1973 [1861]). *Incidents in the Life of a Slave Girl.* Lydia Maria Child (ed.). New York: Harcourt Brace Jovanovich.

Brooks, G. (1997 [1953]). "Maud Martha." In H. L. Gates and N. L. McKay (eds.), *The Norton Anthology of African American Literature.* New York: W. W. Norton.

Burgess, N. J. (1994). "Gender Roles Revisited: The Development of the Woman's Place among African-American Women in the United States." *Journal of Black Studies* 24(4): 391–401.

———. (1995). "Female Headed Households in Sociohistorical Perspective." In B. Dickerson (ed.), *African American Single Mothers,* 21–36. Beverly Hills, CA: Sage.

Cannon, K. G. (1995). *Katie's Cannon: Womanism and the Soul of the Black Community.* New York: Continuum.

Carlson, Shirley J. (1992, Spring). "Black Ideals of Womanhood in the Late Victorian Era." *Journal of Negro History* 77(2): 61–73.

Cheatham, H. E., & Stewart, J. B. (1993). *Black Families.* New Brunswick, NJ: Transaction.

Christian, B. (1985). *Black Feminist Criticism: Perspectives on Black Women Writers.* New York: Pergamon Press.

Coffin, L. (1968 [1876]). *Reminiscences of Levi Coffin.* North Stratford, NH: Ayer Publishing.

Collins, P. H. (1991). "The Meaning of Motherhood in Black Culture." In R. Staples (ed.), *The Black Family: Essays and Studies.* Belmont, CA: Wadsworth.

———. (1998, September). "The Tie that Binds: Race, Gender and U.S. Violence." *Ethnic and Racial Studies* 21: 5.

Connor, K. R. (1994). *Conversions and Visions.* Knoxville: University of Tennessee Press.

Cooper, A. J. (1988 [1892]). *A Voice from the South.* New York: Oxford University Press.

Crabtree, B., & Miller, W. L. (eds.). (1992). *Doing Qualitative Research.* Newbury Park, CA: Sage.

Cross, T. (ed.) (1999/2000, Winter). "From 1977 to 1995 Black Women Steadily Increased their Share of all Doctorates Awarded to African Americans." *Journal of Blacks in Higher Education* 26: 82–85.

———. (2000/2001, Winter). "Black Women Now Dominate African American Law School Enrollments." *Journal of Blacks in Higher Education* 30: 64–66.

———. (2001, Summer). "Black Women are Responsible for Closing College-Educated Racial Income Gap." *Journal of Blacks in Higher Education* 32: 33–34.

———. (2001/2002, Winter). "The Striking Progress of African Americans in Degree Attainments." (Index shows "Black women now earn nearly two thirds of all bachelor's degrees awarded to African Americans.) *Journal of Blacks in Higher Education* 34: 100–106.

Cross, T., & Slater, R. B. (2001, Autumn). "The Troublesome Decline in African American College Student Graduation Rates: The Success of Black Women Compared to Black Men." *Journal of Blacks in Higher Education* 33: 102–109.

Davis, A. (1981). *Women, Race, and Class.* New York: Random House.

———. (1995). "Reflections on the Black Woman's Role in the Community of Slaves." In *Words of Fire, An Anthology of African-American Feminist Thought.* New York: New Press.

Dickerson, B. J. (ed.) (1995). *African American Single Mothers: Understanding Their Lives and Families.* Sage Series on Race and Ethnic Relations, 10. Thousand Oaks, CA: Sage.

Dickson, L. (1993, June). "Future of Marriage and Family." *Journal of Black Studies* 23: 472–491.

Drake, S. C., & Cayton, H. R. (1962 [1945]). *Black Metropolis: A Study of Negro Life in a Northern City.* 2nd ed. New York: Harper Torchbooks.

DuBois, W. E. B. (1989 [1903]). *The Souls of Black Folk.* New York: Penguin.

———. (1969 [1908]). *The Negro American Family.* New York: New American Library.

Edwards, A., & Polite, C. K. (1992). *Children of the Dream: The Psychology of Black Success.* New York: Doubleday.

Ellison, R. (1952). *The Invisible Man.* New York: Random House.

Ervin, H. A. (1999). *African American Literary Criticism, 1773 to 2000.* New York: Twayne.

Fox-Genovese, E. (1988). *Within the Plantation Household: Black and White Women of the Old South.* Chapel Hill: University of North Carolina Press.

Franklin, J. H. (1969). *From Slavery to Freedom.* New York: Random House.

Frazier, E. F. (1930). "The Negro Slave Family." In *Journal of Negro History* 15, 213–41, 244–59.

———. (1966 [1939]). *The Negro Family in the United States.* Chicago: University of Chicago Press.

Gates, H. L., Jr. (gen'l. ed.) (1988). *Six Women's Slave Narratives.* New York: Oxford University Press.

———. (1990). *Reading Black, Reading Feminist: A Critical Anthology.* New York: Penguin Books.

Gates, H. L., Jr., and McKay, N. L. (eds.) (1997). *The Norton Anthology of African American Literature.* New York: W. W. Norton and Co.

Gilbert, S. M., and Gubar, S. (1996). *The Norton Anthology of Literature of Women.* New York: W. W. Norton and Co.

Glaser, B. G., & Strauss, A. L. (1967). *The Discovery of Grounded Theory: Strategies for Qualitative Research.* Chicago: Aldine.

Graham, Maryemma. (1999, Spring). "Margaret Walker: Fully a Poet, Fully a Woman (1915–1998)." *The Black Scholar* 29(2/3): 37–46.

Green-Powell, P. "Methodological Research in Field Research: Six Case Studies." In K. M. Vaz (ed.) *Oral Narrative Research with Black Women.* Thousand Oaks, CA: Sage.

Guba, E. (1978). *Toward a Method of Naturalistic Inquiry in Educational Evaluation.* Los Angeles: Center for the Study of Evaluation.

Guy-Sheftall, B. (ed.) (1998). *Words of Fire. An Anthology of African-American Feminist Thought.* New York: New Press.

Hacker, A. (1992). *Two Nations: Black, White, Separate, Hostile, Unequal.* New York: Scribner's.

Hambrick, A. (1997). "You Haven't Seen Anything Until You Make a Black Woman Mad." In K. M. Vaz (ed.) *Oral Narrative Research with Black Women.* Thousand Oaks, CA: Sage.

Hedrick, J. (1994). *Harriet Beecher Stowe.* New York: Oxford University Press.

Hernton, C. (1965). *Sex and Racism in America.* New York: Grove Press.

Higginbotham, E. "Two Representative Issues in Contemporary Sociological Work on Black Women." Hull, G. T. et al. (1982).

———. (1971). *Coming Together: Black Power, White Hatred, and Sexual Hang-Ups.* New York: Random House.

Hines, D. C. (ed.). (1997). *Encyclopedia of Black Women in American Literature.* New York: Facts on File.

Holloway, K. F. C. (1992). *Moorings and Metaphors: Figures of Culture and Gender in Black Women's* Literature. New Brunswick, NJ: Rutgers University Press.

hooks, b. (1992). *Ain't I a Woman: Black Women and Feminism.* Boston: South End Press.

————. (2000, November). "Learning in the Shadow of Race and Class." In *Chronicle of Higher Education*, B14–16.

Hull, G. T., et al. (eds) (1982). *All the Women Are White, All the Blacks Are Men, but Some of Us Are Brave: Black Women's Studies*. New York: Feminist Press.

Hurston, Z. N. (1997 [1928]). "How It Feels to Be Colored Me." In H. L. Gates, Jr., and N. L. McKay (eds.) *Norton Anthology of African American Literature*. New York: W. W. Norton.

Hymowitz, C., and Weissman, M. (1978). *A History of Women in America from Founding Mothers to Feminists: How Women Shaped the Life and Culture in America*. New York: Bantam Books.

Isenberg, N. (1998). *Sex and Citizenship in Antebellum America*. Chapel Hill: University of North Carolina Press.

Jackson. E. M. (1992). *Images of Black Men in Black Women Writers, 1950–1990*. Bristol, IN: Wyndham Hall Press.

James, Joy (1999, Winter). "Resting in Gardens, Battling in Deserts: Black Women's Activism." *The Black Scholar* 29(4): 2–7.

Jenkins, M. (1999). *The South in Black and White: Race, Sex, and Literature in the 1940s*. Aiken: University of South Carolina Press.

Jones, J. (1985). *Labor of Love, Labor of Sorrow: Black Women, Work and the Family, from Slavery to the Present*. New York: Vintage Books.

Ladner, J. (1972). *Tomorrow's Tomorrow*. New York: Doubleday.

Lerner, G. (ed.) (1992). *Black Women in White America: A Documentary History*. New York: Vintage Books.

Lincoln, Y., & Guba, E. (1985). *Naturalistic Inquiry*. Newbury Park, CA: Sage.

Loguen, J. W. (1859). *The Rev. J. W. Loguen as a Slave and as a Free Man*. Syracuse, NY: Author.

Lourdes, A. (1978). "A Litany for Survival," in *The Black Unicorn*. New York: W. W. Norton.

McAdoo, H. P. (ed.) (1988). *Black Families*. Newbury Park, CA: Sage.

McGill, Lisa D. (2000, Summer). "Thinking Back through the Mother: The Poetics of Place and the Mother/Daughter Dyad in *Brown Girl, Brownstones.*" *The Black Scholar* 30(2)2: 34–40.

McKinney, G. P., Sr., and McKinney, R. I. (1987). *History of the Black Baptists of Florida, 1850–1985*. Miami: Florida Memorial College Press.

Merriam, S. (1988). *Case Study Research in Education: A Qualitative Approach*. Newbury Park, CA: Sage.

Mintz, S. (ed.) (1996). *African American Voices: The Life Cycle of Slavery*. Naugatuck, CT: Brandywine Press.

Moody, J. (1997). "Professions of Faith: A Teacher Reflects on Women, Race, Church, and Spirit." In K. M. Vaz (ed.) *Oral Narrative Research with Black Women*. Thousand Oaks, CA: Sage.

Morrison, T. (1987). *Beloved*. New York: Knopf.

Moynihan, D. P. (1965). *The Negro Family: The Case for National Action*. Washington: U.S. Government Printing Office.

Naylor, G. (1993). *Mama Day*. New York: Random House.

Nettles, M. T. (1997). *The African American Education Data Book*. Fairfax, VA: Frederick D. Patterson Research Institute College Fund/UNCF.

Oakes, J. (1990). *Slavery and Freedom: An Interpretation of the Old South*. New York: Routledge.

Office of Institutional Research (2002). *Fact Book: Gender and ethnic composition of the student body*. Data collected by William E. Hopper, director of institutional research. Miami: Florida Memorial College.

Ojo-Ade, F. (1996). *Of Dreams Deferred, Dead or Alive: African Perspectives on African American Writers.* Westport, CT: Greenwood Press.

Omalade, B. (1994). *The Rising Song of African American Women.* New York: Routledge.

Patton, M. Q. (1987). *How to Use Qualitative Methods in Evaluation.* Newbury Park, CA: Sage.

Peterson, E. A. (1992). *African American Women: A Study of Will and Success.* Jefferson, NC: McFarland.

———. (1997). "African American Women and the Emergence of Self-Will: The Use of Phenomenological Research." In K. M. Vaz (ed.), *Oral Narrative Research with Black Women.* Thousand Oaks, CA: Sage.

Pierce-Baker, C. (1998). *Surviving the Silence: Black Women's Stories of Rape.* New York: W. W. Norton.

Prothrow-Stith, D. (1993). *Deadly Consequences: How Violence Is Destroying Our Teenage Population and a Plan to Begin Solving the Problem.* New York: Harper Perennial.

Redmond, S. P. (1942, April [1862]). "The Negroes in the United States of America." *Journal of Negro History.* 27(2): 216–18, 235.

Robinson-Jacobs, K. (2001, July 15). "Census Finds High Number of Black Female Entrepreneurs." *Los Angeles Times,* C1, C6.

Robnett, B. (1997). *How Long? How Long? African American Women in the Struggle for Civil Rights.* New York: Oxford University Press.

Rodgers-Rose, L. (1996). *Violence against Black Women.* Newark, NJ: Traces Institute Publications/IBWC.

Ross, M. J. (1998). *Success Factors of Young African American Males at a Historically Black College.* Westport, CT: Greenwood Press.

Sardar, Z., and Loon, B. V. (1998). *Cultural Studies.* New York: Totem Books.

Schiller, N. (2000, Autumn). "A Short History of Black Feminist Scholars." *Journal of Blacks in Higher Education* 29, 119–25.

Scott, J. (1993). "African American Daughter-Mother Relations and Teenage Pregnancy: Two Faces of Premarital Pregnancy." *Western Journal of Black Studies,* 2(17): 73–81.

———. (2001, July 29). "Rethinking Segregation beyond Black and White." *New York Times,* 4.

Showalter, E. (1991). *Sister's Choice.* New York: Oxford University Press.

Slater, R. B. (1994). "The Growing Gender Gap in Higher Education." *Journal of Blacks in Higher Education,* 3: 52–59.

Spradley, J. P. (1979). *The Ethnographic Interview.* New York: Holt, Rinehart and Winston.

Staples, R. (ed.) (1991). *The Black Family: Essays and Studies.* Belmont, CA: Sage.

Stone, R. D. (2001, August). "Silent No More." *Essence,* 123–26, 153–56.

Stowe, H. B. (1962 [1852]). *Uncle Tom's Cabin.* New York: Washington Square Press.

Truth, S. (1986 [1852]). "Ain't I a Woman." In S. M. Gilbert and S. Gubar (eds.). *Literature by Women.* New York: W. W. Norton.

Tsurutas, Dorothy Randell. (1999, Spring). "Margaret Walker: Fully a Poet, Fully a Woman (1915–1998)." *The Black Scholar* 29(2/3): 37–46.

Vaz, K. M. (ed.). (1997). *No Crystal Stair: Visions of Race and Gender in Black Women's Fiction.* Cleveland: Pilgrim Press.

———. (1997b). "Social Responsibility and Social Resistance: Women's Perspectives on Women's Place." *Oral Narrative Research with Black Women.* Thousand Oaks, CA: Sage.

Wade-Gayles, G. (1991). "Connected to Mama's Spirit." In P. Bell-Scott & B. Guy-Sheftall (eds.) *Double Stitch: Black Women Write about Mothers and Daughters.* New York: Harper Perennial.

———. (ed.). (1995). *My Soul Is a Witness: African-American Women's Spirituality.* Boston: Beacon Press.

Walcott-Mcquigg, J. A. (1997). "Methodological Issues in Triangulation." In K. M. Vaz (ed.), *Oral Narrative Research with Black Women.* Thousand Oaks, CA: Sage.

Walker, A. (1966). *Jubilee.* Boston: Houghton Mifflin.

———. (1997). "In Search of our Mother's Garden." In H. L. Gates, Jr., and N. L. McKay (eds.) *The Norton Anthology of African American Literature.* New York: W. W. Norton (pp. 2380–2387).

Wallace, M. (1979). *Black Macho and the Myth of the Superwoman.* New York: Dial.

Watkins, M. (2001, Spring). "In Memoriam: Gwendolyn Brooks (1917–2000)." *The Black Scholar* 31(1): 51–54.

Weber, J. (1992). "Creating the Environment for Minority Student Success: An Interview with Jacqueline Fleming." *Journal of Developmental Education* 16: 20–24.

West, C. (1994). *Race Matters.* New York: Vintage.

White, D. G. (1998). *Too Heavy a Load: Black Women in Defense of Themselves, 1894–1994.* New York: W. W. Norton.

———. (1999). *Arn't I a Woman? Female Slaves in the Plantation South.* New York: W. W. Norton.

Williams, R., Jr. (2000). *African American Autobiography and the Quest for Freedom.* Westport, CT: Greenwood Press.

Woodson, C. G. (1916, April). "Slave Advertisements." *Journal of Negro History* 1: 163–216.

———. (1916–). *Journal of Negro History.* (Washington: Association for the Study of Negro Life and History.) 1–53.

Index

ABOUT THE AUTHOR

MARILYN J. ROSS is Professor of Higher Education/English at Florida Memorial College, Miami.